ADVENTURES WITH A SAINT:
Kateri Tekakwitha, "Lily of The Mohawks"

By Marlene McCauley

Grace House Publishing Co.
6237 N. 15th Street
Phoenix, Arizona 85014

i

Adventures With a Saint
Kateri Tekakwitha, "Lily of The Mohawks"

Kateri and Friends at Roma, in Poetry
Registered, April 28, 1989 as:
Diary of a Phoenix Family in Roma
for the Beatification of Kateri Tekakwitha.
Marlene McCauley, TXv 367-108
Library of Congress Copyright Department

Library of Congress Catalog Card Number: 92-071889
ISBN: 0-963633-0-1

Morneau Typographers   Bradley Printers
Phoenix, Arizona

ADVENTURES WITH A SAINT:
Kateri Tekakwitha "Lily of The Mohawks"

By Marlene McCauley

Editor: R. Allan McCauley

Grace House Publishing

Phoenix, Arizona

Other Works by Marlene McCauley

The Pretzel Story (History, Custom, Prayer, Recipe)
An Artist's Farewell (Poetry of Ted DeGrazia's Funeral)
Collection of Poetry (Philosophical, Nature, Whimsical)
The Fatima Story (Drama)
Miracle of the Roses (Drama)
Lily of the Mohawks (Children's Puppet Drama)
Children's Biography of Kateri, soon to be published

Video: McCauley Family "Puppets & Moppets"
Two 30-minute Productions for Children
1. "Circus on Strings"
2. "Lily of the Mohawks"

Inquiries to:
Grace House Publishing
6237 N. 15th St.
Phoenix, Arizona
85014

Dedication

To my dear mother,
husband and six children

To our spiritual father,
the late Rev. Francis X. Weiser, S.J.

To the late Vice-Postulators
Rev. Joseph McBride, S.J. (United States)
Rev. Henri Béchard, S.J. (Canada)

To all our Native American
and other friends of Kateri
United in the Hearts of Jesus & Mary
and especially to our precious Kateri
Tekakwitha, "Lily of the Mohawks."

Acknowledgements

My sincere gratitude is expressed to the multitude of friends who were tremendously supportive in behalf of this work for Kateri without whose help, it could not have been accomplished.

Heartfelt appreciation to the dedicated typists: Sherry Welsch, Eileen Thompson, Rita Zimney and Jim Woodley as well as to those friends who gave invaluable professional input: John Barger of Sophia Press, Alice Von Hildebrand, Ph.D. (Philosopher, Author, Professor Emeritus—Hunter College), William Marra, Ph.D. (Fordham University). Gratitude to those friends who contributed photography, namely: Anne Scheureman (Kateri photographer & Prof. of Monroe College, N.Y.); to Fathers Ronald Sams, S.J., and Simon Conrad, O.F.M. I am also indebted to Father Thomas Egan, S.J. for the valuable time he spent proofreading, and to Allan, my husband, who edited with great dedication.

May Kateri smile upon the following friends and family members who have helped prayerfully, financially or otherwise:

Anne Scheureman, Mary-Eunice Spagnola, Dick Egan, Jean McCauley, Edna and Peter McCauley Family, Josephine Stocklosa, Rev. J. Walter Stocklosa, Anonymous Angel, Rita and Bill Nagle, Helen and Fred Brown, Jean and Peter Robaczewski, Dick and Phyllis McCollum, Katheleen and Gerry McCarthy Family, Marcia Scully, Bob Callary, Irene and Gerry Ross Family, Lillian and Charles Garbarini Family, Sr. Katheleen Jacobsen, Dr. Solomon and Mary Cook, the Albert Lazarre Family, Sr. Michelle Edwards of the Precious Blood, C.S.G.S., Cherri and Katrino Gomez Family, David and Joan Kelly Family, Barney and Helen Wojnarowski Family, Jack and Marie Baker Family, John and Barbara Moran Family, Bob and Sophia Munson Family, Gerard and Louise Quinn Family, Dr. Charles and Mary Ellis Family, Dr. Robert and Dorothy Westfall Family, The John Barger Family, Josephine Johnson, John and Alice Jess Families, Alice Von Hildebrand, Ph.D., William Marra, Ph.D., Rev. Roger McAulife, S.J., Brother Raymond Bounds, S.J., Arnold and Nancy Sodikoff Family, Alma and Meghan Bailey, Mike Surrarrer, Luigi and Ada Desideri Family, Cecilia Katsumato, Chet Adams, The Frank Snyder Family, Ella Stears Family, Nellie Jenulis, Laura Monette, Annie Collette, Amelia Senten, Rita Farley, Peg Schirmer, Larry and Marie Schmitt Family, Ray Boley, Barbara and Bill Magner, Katherine Tesoriero, Mary Long, Anna Fox, Virginia Bache, Mabel Mellena.

I shower my love and appreciation to my precious widowed mother, Laura Monette, in whose home in Nahant, Mass., hours were spent typing and re-typing manuscripts while she provided great love, devotion and fabulous cooking, so her daughter could work in behalf of the family's favorite, "Babe of the Woods," Kateri Tekakwitha. To my darling husband, Allan, my eternal companion who spent hours over a two year period, editing scripts in various coffee shops around Phoenix, during breaks from his legal practice. To my loving six children for their encouragement and prayers and to our darling grandchildren.

To ALL: THANK YOU...GOD BLESS YOU FOREVER!

Table of Contents

PART ONE

Individual Accounts of Kateri's Enormous Heart

Prayer and A Peaceful Death

Table of Contents (Continued)

Kateri's Beloved Priests

A Story of Doves

PART TWO

Early Days: Home to Rome

PART THREE

Kateri and Friends At Roma

*Poetic Account
of the
Seven Day Pilgrimage to Rome
June 19 — June 26
1980*

*To witness a great moment in history
when an Iroquois virgin from
the Eastern woodland
of newborn America
received her crown
as "Blessed"*

Table of Contents (Continued)

PART FOUR

Later Days: Rome to Home

APPENDICES

"Lily of the Mohawks," Puppet Production

Francis Xavier, Thomas More, Mary, Anne, Peter

Letter From Father Thomas F. Egan, S.J.

Dear Reader:

It was late summer 1975 when I first met the McCauley family—Allan and Marlene, easterners who had migrated to the Southwest with their children, Francis Xavier and Mary in their high school years, Thomas More and Annie, exuberant like the younger Bobbsey twins, and five year old Peter whom a childhood sickness had left without the sense of hearing. Marlene's professor from college days, Father F.X. Weiser, S.J., had told the family to pray to Kateri Tekakwitha, the seventeenth-century Mohawk maiden whose cause for sainthood had been begun and whose story he had told a few years before in a book on her life. Pray the family did and soon Peter could hear again. It was in thanksgiving for this cure that the McCauleys had accepted the invitation by another Jesuit, Father Joseph S. McBride, to present their play about Kateri at the place of her birth, Auriesville, New York, where the Martyrs Shrine now stands. I felt the family had adopted me the very night of their arrival. Next morning I was careening around the grounds with Tom and Annie in a decrepit golf cart.

The next year I was on hand for another presentation by the family at the Eucharistic Congress in Philadelphia. Joseph Ignatius had been born just three days before curtain call. Marlene, always one to improvise, brought her tiny infant on stage as the baby Kateri asleep in her arms. The following Saturday, after the Mohawk people from Kahnawake had sung the mass in their own language in historic St. Joseph's Church, Joseph was baptized by Father McBride. The McCauleys came to Auriesville for two more years, but then as the older children went off to college, a wonderful playlet with live characters blended with puppets had to be put aside. All good things in this world come to an end.

I was reunited with the McCauleys, at least the parents and their two youngest sons, on the pilgrimage to Rome when Kateri was made a blessed by Pope John Paul II. Through my present work among the Mohawk people of St. Regis I have had the good fortune on several occasions to visit the family in their home in north Phoenix, along with the late Father Henri Béchard, S.J. and Brother Bertrand Girard, S.J. Their oldest daughter Mary now has a family of her own and young Joseph is almost ready for college. Yet to the many who have come to know the McCauleys, they remain a remarkable Christian family, united through the strong bonds of charity, concerned for those in need, strongly motivated by their Catholic faith. May the Lord continue to bless them and help them working together for His greater glory.

Thomas F. Egan, S.J.
Pastor, St. Regis Mission
Former Director, Martyrs Shrine

Marlene in role of "Meadow" (Kateri's mother)
Babe Joseph plays Babe Kateri (called "Sunshine")

Three Missionaries:
(Fathers James de Lamberville, Bruyas and Pierron)
Francis Xavier, McC.; Thomas More, McC.; Peter McCauley

Pope John Paul II
Photo: Anne Scheureman

The Church has declared to the world that Kateri Tekakwitha is blessed; that she lived a life on earth of exemplary holiness and that she is now a member in Heaven of the Communion of Saints who continually intercede with the merciful Father on our behalf....

....Pope John Paul II
addressing the faithful
at the Beatification of
Kateri Tekakwitha
June 1980—Vatican City

FOREWORD

Monsignor Paul A. Lenz
Executive Director
Bureau of Catholic Indian Missions
Washington, D.C.

ROME, THE ETERNAL CITY, as so many writers have described the beautiful metropolis that surrounds the Vatican, seemingly has different meanings for every person. Some admire the history of the age old city, others the beauty of the masterpieces of art and sculpture, many are enthralled with the centuries of the Catholic Church, of the Popes, Councils, doctrines and all that goes with the administration of the largest Church organization in the world. I have visited the Vatican and Rome quite a few times. A very memorable occasion was the Beatification of Blessed Kateri Tekakawitha in June of 1980. As the Director of the Bureau of Catholic Indian Missions for the United States, I was one of the leaders for the activities of the Beatification. Prior to the pilgrimage to Rome I helped organize the liturgical and social activities that are part of such a great event. Then in Rome I was privileged to mingle with many religious from the United States and Canada, as well as Native Americans and laity making up the pilgrimage gathering. The McCauley family of Phoenix — how happy I was to meet and be with Allan, Marlene and children. Just being in the presence of the McCauleys was uplifting, for I was, as everyone else, aware of their devotion to Blessed Kateri and through her, to the Church.

The day before the Beatification, the President of the United States, Jimmy Carter, was at the Vatican to visit the Holy Father and we pilgrims were invited to attend a special audience with the Holy Father and President Carter. As I occupied a place of honor with the dignitaries in my capacity as Bureau Director, I looked around to see how I could assist people present to greet and shake the hands of the Holy Father and President Carter. One of those spotted was Peter McCauley. Enlightened as to how things get done on such an occasion, I was able to arrange for Peter McCauley to be one of those privileged persons — to greet both Pope John Paul II and President Jimmy Carter. The McCauleys were deeply affected by the Beatification of Blessed Kateri as were so many others, Indians and non-Indians. I work with and visit Native Americans all over the United States and I believe the greatest miracle of Blessed Kateri is how she has, since the ceremony at the Vatican June 22, 1980, come into the lives and homes of Native Americans all over the continent.

Years ago when I was a missionary in Paraguay, South America, I noticed the photos of Pope John XXIII and President John Kennedy in the homes of the people. Now here in the States I am seeing the photos of Pope John Paul II and Blessed Kateri everywhere in homes. They are strong bonds of spiritual unification for Native Americans everywhere. Blessed Kateri is being received by the people and especially by the youth, as the youthful Peter and the McCauley Family were inspired by Blessed Kateri. *Adventures with a Saint: Kateri Tekakwitha, "Lily of the Mohawks"* tells this so well! Let it be our prayer that other families and youth will likewise be motivated through the beautiful and meaningful work of Marlene McCauley.

The following is an excerpt
taken from a letter of Father Pierre Cholenec,
one of Kateri's spiritual advisors,
on the death of the holy maiden,
written, May 1, 1680:

*"She died as she lived, that is to say
as a saint.
Such she was regarded here by all the village
before and after her death ..."*

Positio, Fordham Press
New York, 1940

Shortly after Kateri's death,
a granite tombstone was erected over her gravesite
which contains the following inscription:

KATERI TEKAKWITHA

April 17, 1680

Onkwe Onwe-ke Katsitsiio Teiotsitsianekaron

*(Kateri Tekakwitha, the most beautiful flower
that bloomed among the Indians).*

Preface
Marlene McCauley

We invite you to begin, *Adventures With a Saint* by following Kateri Tekakwitha's path to holiness, originating in the recesses of her magnanimous heart. It is then that you will encounter the depth of her love for *you* as an individual which you will discover is as *brilliant* and *burning* as the Arizona sunshine and as deep as the Grand Canyon. You will feel Kateri's presence so much so that you will wish to embrace her.

May this humble work, bring you to a closer union with Christ, through the burning ardor Kateri had for Christ and His cross, from which flowed her boundless love for mankind.

The following is a glimpse into Kateri's life...then follows a kaleidoscope of accounts which will help you observe the intercessory powers of this dynamic saintly maiden, in action, in our era.

Turn the page to begin an adventure with a saint. Join Kateri and her friends....reliving her path to holiness.......

© 1985, Marlene McCauley, Phoenix, Arizona
"Lily of the Mohawks" Bronze 6,
(Photo: Linda Robb)

Cradled by a heavy cross,
Alone without her kin,
Heart-pierced with bitter loss,
Left dark by vision dim.

The Story of Kateri Tekakwitha

Kateri's story is how she blossomed as a "lily" amidst the hardships that surrounded her. Kateri Tekakwitha was born in Ossernenon, New York (now Auriesville) in 1656, the daughter of an Algonquin Christian mother. Her father was a Mohawk Chief of the Turtle clan. A smallpox epidemic left Tekakwitha orphaned at four, with impaired vision and deep pock-marks on her face. She was adopted by an uncle, also one of the Mohawk Chiefs.

Tekakwitha was known for her beautiful artistry at bead-work, embroidery and weaving, while always working cheerfully and industriously. Throughout her life she resisted marriage, choosing ultimately to have Jesus as her only Spouse. After her Baptism Easter Sunday, April 18, 1676, Kateri was persecuted by her clan, but offered her suffering up for her sins and those of her people in the name of Jesus. In 1677, Kateri Tekakwitha escaped to the newly formed Christian village in Canada, where Indians of all tribes, Algonquins, Hurons, Iroquois, etc., who had often been fiercest enemies, lived as brothers at the "Sault-St. Louis" on the St. Laurence, deeply loving one another, living the Gospel of Christ in perfect charity. There she offered her body to Christ on the cross and her soul to Christ in the Holy Eucharist. Her rosary beads took the place of her Indian beads. She took the vow of chastity on March 25, 1679 on the feast of the Annunciation.

Kateri's love for God manifested itself in a life of prayer, severe penances and acts of charity for the sick and poor of her village. Kateri gave away her good clothing to the poor and had to borrow a dress from her friend, Teresa, for the occasion of receiving the Blessed Sacrament on her deathbed. Some of her sacrifices, included: burning her skin with a firebrand, wearing a hairshirt, sleeping on thorns and kneeling barefoot on snow for hours praying before a crudely carved cross on a tree. When Kateri's spiritual director cautioned her to stop excessive penances, explaining that God did not expect her to abuse herself for Him, she obeyed, continuing sacrifices of a lesser degree.

"Kateri received the good news that she might make her First Communion on Christmas Day 1677 with all imaginable joy...She approached herself to this furnace of sacred love that burns on our altars, and came out of it so glowing with this divine fire that only Our Lord knew what had passed between Himself and His dear spouse during her First Communion. All that we can say is that from that day forward she appeared different from us, because she remained so full of God and of love of Him."

— Fr. Pierre Cholenec, S.J.
Extract from Jesuit Relations

IMPORTANT DATES IN KATERI'S LIFE

1656   Kateri Tekakwitha is born at Ossernenon, today, Auriesville, N.Y.

1660   An epidemic of smallpox takes the lives of Kateri's mother, father and brother. Her uncle and aunts adopt her.

1667   Three Jesuit missionaries visit her village of Ossernenon and spend three days there.

1670   Fr. Francis Boniface comes to live at the village.

1675   Fr. James de Lamberville is appointed as Fr. Boniface's successor.

1676   Kateri Tekakwitha is baptized by Fr. de Lamberville.

1677   In October, Kateri escapes to the Mission of St. Francis Xavier on the St. Lawrence River near Montreal.

1677   Kateri makes her first holy Communion on Christmas Day.

1678   On Easter Sunday, Kateri is admitted to the Confraternity of the Holy Family.

1679   Kateri takes the vow of perpetual virginity on March 25, feast of the Annunciation.

1680   Kateri Tekakwitha dies on April 17, Wednesday of Holy Week.

1680   Kateri appears to Fr. Chauchetiere on Easter Monday.

1680   She appears to Anastasia, her second mother.

1680   She also appears to her friend Marie Theresa Tegaiaguenta.

1681   On September 1, she appears a second time to Fr. Chauchetiere.

1682   On April 21, she appears a third time to Fr. Chauchetiere.

1682   During March, the first novena made to Kateri results in the cure of an Indian woman.

1939   The Cause for the canonization of Kateri Tekakwitha is accepted by the Congregation of Rites.

1943   Pope Pius XII formally declares the virtues of Kateri heroic, thereby giving her the title of "Venerable."

1980   Pope John Paul II beatifies Kateri Tekakwitha.

Kateri Tekakwitha's life exemplified a pilgrim soul who lived the cross as a child, embraced the cross after her Baptism and died in the light of the holy cross on Wednesday of Holy Week, April 17, 1680, with the words, "Jesus, Mary," promising to pray for her friends from Heaven, advising them to continue praying and practicing penance. Providentially, Kateri died the day before two feasts of her great loves: Holy Thursday, when Christ instituted Holy Eucharist and Good Friday. Kateri died at twenty-four, resplendently beautiful as her pock-marked skin became ivory smooth in its transfiguration. 'Tekakwitha,' is interpreted as "bumping-or-stumbling-into-things," "pushing-ones-way-through or clearing the path." However, since Kateri bumped, stumbled and pushed her way through adversity until she found God, we can safely say that Kateri Tekakwitha leads all to God by her good example, thus giving her name a new dimension: "she-who-puts-things-in-order!"

These facts recorded in the *Jesuit Relations*, the official daily journal of the Jesuits, was a precursor of many wonderful things yet to unfold about this heroic Indian maiden. After an intensive investigation into her life, she was declared "Venerable" by Pope Pius XII, in 1943, which meant that she had passed "phase one" of a three tiered incredibly tough journey toward canonization...but more about this later.

© Marlene McCauley
Phoenix, Arizona
1992

Radiant soul... God's bride,
Lost herself to find,
Him... wherein all life abide,
To love and serve mankind.

Allan, Marlene, Francis Xavier, Thomas More, Mary, Anne, Peter

Author's Note

The following letter was written to the students of St. John's Indian Mission by the late Vice-Postulator of America, Father Joseph McBride, S.J., known by the Mohawk Indians as "Chief Beautiful Blue Skies." It was read before our family's puppet-drama, *Lily of the Mohawks,* presented on the occasion of the 300th anniversary of Kateri's Baptism, April 18, 1976 at St., John's, Phoenix, Arizona, when our precious Iroquois Princess was still "Venerable."

OSSERNENON

Auriesville, New York

March 28, 1976

Office of
Vice-Postulator

Dear Students of St. John's Mission,

Today you are very fortunate to learn the story of the Indian Maiden known as the Venerable Kateri Tekakwitha. The great thing about this young girl is that she lived in a time when there were many, many difficulties preventing any one from becoming a Christian. Yes, she was a true Mohawk Indian true to all the grand heritage of her people. Her people believed in the Great Spirit and when they listened to the missionaries talk about God and His teachings about creation and the world, they found many similarities. Some found it hard to give up practices that weren't really Christian; others were ready to forsake whatever was superstition and pagan and sought to be baptized by the Jesuit priests who had come from France to work among the Indians of Eastern New York State and the regions of Canada around Montreal.

When Kateri became a Christian she had to endure ridicule and insults for the way she fervently practiced her faith. She escaped from the village where she was baptized on Easter Sunday three hundred years ago and went to Canada where she lived a holy Christian life until she died at twenty-four in 1680. Her holiness has come down to us and we find her the model of all who follow Jesus. She loved the Mass, had a great devotion to Jesus in the Holy Eucharist, did penance for her sins and those of her people, helped to tend the sick and the dying, and prayed fervently to the Great Spirit many hours during the day. All her fine qualities have won for her the title KAIATANORON — "A Lady of Quality" given her by her present day brothers and sisters which were inscribed on her tomb in Caughnawaga, Canada. She still inspires many because of the beautiful life she lived. All over the world she is today admired and loved. Please try to know her better so that you will realize what a great friend you have in heaven from the first Americans who dwelt in our country. Pray to her often and put your needs before her. Pray, too, that miracles will happen through her so that the Church will grant her the honors of beatification and canonization.

Enjoy your show and take with you the spirit Kateri has given to so many especially those of her own race!

Cordially always,

Joseph S. McBride, S.J.

Prayerfully sang the rosary bead,
To spread God's love among,
From this saintly flower seed,
A pristine lily sprung.

The poem, "Lily of the Mohawks," written in 1976, commemorating Kateri's Baptism, paints a picture of the Iroquois virgin who gave her life after her conversion to her one and only Spouse, Jesus Christ to live happily forever in His eternal Kingdom.

"Lily of the Mohawks"

Daughter of the turtle clan,
Seed of martyr's blood,
Embryo of infant land,
Bloom from sacred bud.

Cradled by a heavy cross,
Alone without her kin,
Heart-pierced with bitter loss,
Left dark by vision dim.

Uprooted from her mother earth,
Transplant to pagan soil,
Marred face could naught hide her mirth,
As nimble hands did toil.

Blind to worldy ways around,
In darkness saw a light,
Found peace in war drums' serpent sound,
Blackrobes brought new sight.

Rawennio . . . God of love,
Echoed midst the blight.
Cleansed by water and His dove,
Her soul did soar full height.

A cross weighted with abuse,
Lightened by an angel sigh,
Scorned . . . by her own accused,
Reborn . . . to never die.

The clandestine moon cast its spell,
As shadows stole away,
Kateri bid a sad farewell,
To see a better day.

Through virgin path the trio fled,
By foot and then canoe,
To a distant field where lambs did tread,
Happiness shone anew.

Prayerfully sang the rosary bead,
To spread God's love among,
From this saintly flower seed,
A pristine lily sprung.

Barefoot babe of winter wood,
To the cross of bark did trod,
Enduring pain as great she could,
Adoring Son of God.

Radiant soul . . . God's bride,
Lost herself to find,
Him . . . wherein all life abide,
To love and serve mankind.

Just before her soul took flight,
She picked a sweet bouquet,
Of thoughts for you . . . so pure and white,
"From heaven I will pray!"

Her rosy lips now ashen hue,
When the Angel came to call,
Sighed, "Jesus, Mary, I love you,"
A song sublime for all!.

Soon this fragile flower fell,
Midway in passiontide,
A glow transfiguring her face did tell,
That Christ was at her side.

Kateri Tekakwitha,
Precious gift to man,
Oh, "Lily of the Mohawks,"
Breathe fragrance on our land!

© Marlene McCauley
Phoenix, Arizona
1974

The Cross on which Christ came alive
for St. Francis of Assisi

PART I

Individual Accounts of Kateri Tekakwitha's Enormous Heart For Mankind's Needs

Peter's Miracle of Hearing

On my birthday, September 5, 1968, we were blessed by the birth of a beautiful baby boy, named after a great man, "Peter the Apostle." From the earliest days of his birth, he was a sheer delight, having an enormous smile for everyone he saw. He responded to all of God's little creatures with great love and enthusiasm. He was truly an adorable, gentle soul.

In his fourth year, Peter developed repeated ear infections which did not respond medically, ultimately producing a major hearing deficit in both ears. So bad was the problem that we had to take the TV away for he'd sit about six inches away from the "box" with the volume to its maximum level. When we realized our general practitioner was getting no where with this problem, he was seen by two ear specialists, both of whom confirmed that surgery was the only recourse; the prognosis was not favorable for full recovery with the surgery.

Very shortly after the last doctor's visit, surgery was scheduled for ten days later. At this time, our spiritual father, F. X. Weiser, S.J., my Philosophy Professor and amateur archaeologist was visiting us as part of a lecture series in the Southwest. When he learned of Peter's hearing problem, he said with a thick Austrian accent,

> "We must pray to Kateri Tekakwitha, she NEVER leaves a prayer unanswered!"

We made a novena to Kateri and on the ninth day, which was Holy Wednesday and Kateri's feast day, Peter heard perfectly in both ears and has had perfect hearing ever since! Peter has been an underwater sports enthusiast and just recently has taken the exam for Medical School. But more about Peter later in "Early Days..........

Peter
Heaven's Angel

Kateri: A Friend in Need

Kateri is truly a friend in need. She is unique in that she does accept gifts in exchange for healings. There are several ways she may get to you...in a dream, a vision or an interior voice. If she speaks to you interiorly, do as she instructs. Whatever the situation, Kateri's charm will melt the most hardened heart.

In the Iroquois culture, the Indians believed in dreams to such an extent that they would execute whatever was dictated. Kateri is known to use dreams in a good way.

One such case involves an Uncle who was about to ruin his marriage by alcoholism. One morn, he startled all of us by asking for a medal of Kateri. "She appeared to me in a dream last night and told me to stop drinking!" From that moment on, he lost all desire to drink, attributing his transformation to his, "little babe in the woods!"

To this day, he has worn his Kateri medal faithfully and has never once, in these many years lapsed from his solemn pledge.

With the extra money from not drinking, he and his wife have taken trips to St. Martinique and Barbados. Once Kateri's sweet voice directed me to send him a medal which I did unaware he was away. When he returned and opened the envelope to find a new medal, he was so grateful because he had just lost his only one on the island!

Spiritual Healing

Our dear Aunt Anne was diagnosed as having uterine cancer in 1961. Her doctor gave her only two years to live but as it worked out, he died two years later. As time passed, her condition became critical until by 1973, a tumor, the size of a grapefruit jutted out from her left side.

Shortly thereafter, our family made a pilgrimage to Kateri's shrine in Kahnawake, Canada, in thanksgiving for our son Peter's hearing cure as well as to pray for a physical and spiritual healing for our wonderful auntie. Knowing that she had been separated from the church for sixty years, we begged Kateri to bring her back. Miraculously, within the following year, Aunt Anne's strength returned, her spirits soared and best of all, she was reconciled to our dear Lord on the feast of His Sacred Heart, 1974.

After her confession, all alone in the church, she knelt before the crucifix, (Kateri's special love). With tears gushing from her eyes, she spoke to Christ with all the love from her soul:

> "Why, Lord, didn't I ever go to You with my troubles? I thought I could handle life's problems all by myself and I've had nothing but bad luck... Please forgive me, Lord!"

When leaving the church, she exclaimed, "I feel as light as a feather, like I could fly!"

Aunt Anne lived in fair health for the following seven years but above all she experienced tranquility and spiritual well being having been reconciled to God and His church. She died peacefully on the feast of the Guardian Angels, Oct. 2, 1981. We feel certain that our dear Kateri and her guardian angel escorted our aunt to heaven.

A NEW Foot!

Once when my mother injured her foot from a fall, causing excruciating pain and the need for crutches, we were about to have her x-rayed for fear of a fractured metatarsal. We prayed to Kateri, holding the relic to her foot. I then left to do an errand and found myself making a proposal to Kateri. "If you heal mom's foot, I'll write that article about you!" I had an opportunity to write about Kateri in an International publication but had decided to put the assignment on the "back burner" until more time was available.

Upon returning, I noticed that the injured foot had "wings," for the bed-ridden lovely lady was now up and around, exclaiming, "I have a NEW foot!" Minutes later, with shoes comfortably on, she was "as good as new!" Kateri had accepted the deal; the article was written and published!

A Perfect Thumb

Later that same year, Allan's right thumb became swollen for an extended period, getting progressively more painful and restricted. He finally decided to see his friend, an orthopedic surgeon, but first we agreed that we would pray to Kateri while blessing his thumb with her relic.

Following the prayer, I left to spend an hour with Jesus at an adoration chapel, emulating Kateri's practice of some three hundred years earlier. When returning home, Allan approached me waving his new deflated thumb! The problem has never recurred.

Kateri's Guardian Angel

After arriving from Rome, following Kateri's beatification, enroute from New York to Arizona, the McCauleys were stranded for Sunday Mass in the vast expanse of desert in New Mexico.

Recalling that when Kateri was on the Winter hunt, she would send her guardian angel to attend Mass for her so that he could bring back the graces, we asked Kateri to get her guardian angel to ask *our* guardian angel to help us find a Mass.

The prayer was answered immediately for we were guided to a dilapidated rectory where a forlorn priest stood in desperation because his car broke down and he had no way of getting to his mission church. We practically kissed him and told him of our prayer. He was delighted to hear of Kateri's beatification.

Soon we found ourselves amidst beautiful Mexican people in their tiny house of God in the middle of the desert. At the homily, the priest called me to relate the story of Kateri and her beatification ceremony in Rome. The story began with our first encounter with Kateri through our son's hearing cure.

After Mass, the people assembled outside for questions. We passed out medals, prints and literature. We knew Kateri's angel escorted our angel who lead us into the desert to proclaim the good news of the humble Iroquois Virgin who just received her "Blessed" crown!

Kateri Illumines a Soul

"Cleansed by Water and His Dove, her soul did soar full height"

Our niece, Ilene McCauley, an attorney from Mesa, Arizona, always had a deep love for God which was instilled in her during childhood by her dear Jewish mother who had been confined to a wheelchair with multiple sclerosis. Unfortunately, all the love she possessed was totally shattered by severe marital problems which began in 1983. In March of 1984, when Ilene felt totally abandoned and cried continually, Allan and I gave her a medal of Kateri which she wore faithfully. In August, 1984, when the Tekakwitha Conference was held in Phoenix, we had a get together at our home. Many Native American and non-Indian friends came, including missionary priest, Father Thomas Egan, S.J. who blessed Ilene with Kateri's relic.

In the months following, while the marital situation was worsening and depression increasing, Ilene never removed her medal. On the eve of Nov. 23 of the same year, as she was leaving her law office, she inhaled a breathtaking aroma of roses in the parking lot, though Ilene was certain there were no roses anywhere. That evening, an incredible phenomenon took place. As Ilene entered her dark laundry room, she was instantly startled by a flash of brilliant light which filled the area. Terrified, she saw centered in the circle of light, a smiling face with long braids. Her fear was replaced by a strange inexplicable warmth and feeling of well being. Ilene explained, "In a flash, the light and image disappeared." At that moment of brilliant light, another light filled her soul, a light of faith and joyful acceptance that whatever happened would be right and good for God would take care of her.

Soon thereafter, Ilene called to tell us how Kateri came to help her. Though Kateri didn't verbally speak to Ilene, she caused something to happen which changed her entire outlook. She knew at that moment that she wanted to be baptized a Roman Catholic.

On Jan. 1, 1985 (feast of Mary, Mother of Hope) Ilene called Monsignor Neil McHugh to ask for instructions in the faith. Like Kateri when she was a catechumen, Ilene understood everything with extraordinary clarity. Monsignor McHugh was amazed that she never doubted any aspect of the faith.

As Kateri was baptized on Easter, so was Ilene; Allan and I were delighted to have been invited to be her Godparents. Ilene had grown to love the Blessed Mother and her rosary just as Kateri did. She took "Katharine Mary" as her confirmation name.

Since Kateri appeared to Ilene, that November evening of 1983, her life has fallen into place like a beautiful design. Recently, Ilene was awarded "The Outstanding Young Lawyer Award for 1991," for her community service involving aid to youth, a program which has since spread throughout the U.S. Ilene's new positive outlook, resulting from a rebirth within her soul, was evoked by a little Indian maiden whose prayers and sacrifices of over three hundred years ago, gave her great intercessory power from Heaven. Kateri Tekakwitha loves Ilene and came to keep her promise, made from her deathbed, that she would help her friends from Heaven. Coincidentally, Ilene's birthday falls on June 22, the day Kateri was beatified as well as on the feast of another lawyer, St. Thomas More. Ilene concluded, "Out of this experience has risen a deeper love and trust in God than I ever thought possible as well as tremendous personal satisfaction and confidence. I am ever grateful to Kateri Tekakwitha for these blessings."

Though Ilene had never read accounts of Kateri's apparitions, it is written in the *Positio*,* Fordham Press, N.Y., 1940 that such similar occurrences took place shortly after Kateri's death. One biographer, Father Peter Cholenec, S.J., who had been one of Kateri's spiritual directors, wrote in his *Life of Katharine Tegakowitha, First Iroquois Virgin,* 1696: ''The sixth day after Katharine's death, the Monday after Easter, a person of virtue and worthy of belief was praying at 4:00 a.m., when Katharine appeared to him surrounded by glory with majestic bearing and shining face....'' (This person to whom Kateri appeared was another of her spiritual directors, Fr. Claude Chauchétiere, S.J.) It is also recorded that Kateri appeared in brilliant light to her second mother, Anastastia whom she counseled, ''The cross was the glory of my life and death and I encourage you to make it yours.'' Kateri was preparing Anastastia for several major crosses which occurred a short time after the vision —

> *Just before her soul took flight,*
> *She picked a sweet bouquet,*
> *Of thoughts for you so pure and bright.*
> *From Heaven I will pray —*

*A collection of original writings which were used for the introduction of Kateri's cause, all of which are traceable back to her time.

Kateri Leaves No Prayer Unanswered

Our dear Father Weiser always said, "Kateri leaves *no* prayer unanswered." However, since he had not been let out of Campion Center infirmary, Weston, Mass., for four years, because of illness, he knew he would not be able to attend our 25th wedding anniversary which was to be held in Nahant, Mass., a small peninsula, Northeast of Boston, where my parents resided. It was there, where my painting "Kateri's Children of the World," was created.

Father Weiser promised to offer a Mass for us in his room on that special day. After reminding him of his words, "Kateri leaves *no* prayer unanswered," Allan and I invited Father to join us in a novena, invoking Kateri's intercession that he be allowed to attend. We recalled with joy how wonderful it was twenty-five years earlier, when Father Weiser concelebrated our wedding Mass at St. Malachy's, the actor's chapel in New York with Father Ed Sullivan, the circus priest, (whom I had befriended when performing for Ringling Bros. Circus). Kateri couldn't let us down! Two days before the event, he called to say, "My Doctor will let me go!" This was truly a gift from Kateri! We arranged for several Notre Dame nuns (my former teachers from Emmanuel College) to pick him up.

"Marlene, Allan and Joseph with Father F.X. Weiser, S.J."

There he was, seated on the altar at St. Thomas Aquinas Church with a cane. With him concelebrating were: Fathers Joseph McBride, S.J. and Henri Béchard, S.J. (Vice-Postulators); Thomas Egan, S.J. and Robert Fleig, S.J., (Pastor & Assistant of St. Regis Mohawk Parish, Akwesasne, Quebec). Father J. Walter Stocklosa, Pastor, St. Thomas Aquinas Church, (who received the 1991 Kateri Award for his tireless efforts promoting Kateri) and Bishop John J. Mulcahy of Boston, main celebrant, (who helped locate several of the children for my painting of Kateri 1974).

Angel with a Tilted Halo
(Joseph, Age Three)

The Mass was in honor of Blessed Kateri, for the intention that family life be Christ-centered throughout the world. It was the source for some great talks about Kateri who must have smiled when five year old Joseph, standing atop of a stool to reach the microphone, for the reading of one of the intentions, blurted, "That Kateri Tekakwitha becomes a saint, we pray to the Lord!" His loud voice and clear enunciation evoked many smiles throughout the Church, but especially by Father McBride who had baptized Joseph when he was but three days old during the Eucharistic Congress in Philadelphia, 1976, after a Mass honoring Kateri at the old St. Joseph's Church. At the end of our Mass, Bishop Mulcahy presented Father Béchard with a plaque celebrating his 50th year as a Jesuit.

Ringling Bros. Training Ground
Sarasota, Florida
(Marlene on Elephant)

The theme of the party after Mass was, "25 years a Happy Circus!" with balloons, clowns, puppets and "Ruthie," the 9,000 lb. African elephant as the star performer. (Coincidentally, "Ruthie" was the name of the elephant I rode for Ringling Bros. Circus.)

Atop of "Ruthie" Ringling's Elephant
(Marlene in Center Ring)
1957

*Wearing "Kateri Stoles"
(by "Little Peacock")
Father Tom Egan, S.J.
Pastor, St. Regis Mission,
Akwesasne (meaning
"Where-the-partridge-
spreads-its-wings"), Quebec*

*J. Walter Stocklosa, "The Polish Indian"
former pastor, St. Thomas Aquinas Church
Nahant (meaning "Twin Islands"), Mass.*

"Marriage is like Riding an Elephant"
Marlene, Allan and Joseph
25th Anniversary

Since "Ruthie" wasn't the typical pet one would see on Nahant's peninsula, the Associated Press came to do a story... a chance for the McCauleys to plug Kateri and family values. When asked, "Why an elephant for your anniversary?" The answer:

> "Marriage is like riding an elephant! It is an enormous undertaking which calls for holding on tenaciously, meriting the reward of *center ring,* ensuring a loving relationship with God, family and spouse."

To this, Daddy Allan replied with a twinkle in his eye,

> "Nonsense, marriage is psychosis and this is all part of it!" (pointing to elephant)

On August 24, 1992, the McCauleys will have celebrated their 35th! ("time for a herd of elephants!"), while the new Canadian Vice-Postulator, Father Jacques Bruyère, S.J. will have celebrated his 50th!

Since our "25th," God took Fathers Weiser, Fleig, McBride and Béchard to Heaven, to celebrate a gala party with Kateri, and her friends to help hasten her sainthood!

May Kateri Smile Upon You

Kateri had a beautifully cheerful disposition and a great sense of humor while on earth. After death, she did not lose these great traits. The following episode occurred at the Kateri shrine of St. Francis Xavier Church in Phoenix which houses the featureless De Grazia statue.

The bronze of Kateri actually took on features. As Kateri's face became transfigured at her death, so she allowed this face to become alive with expression for a Papago* Indian, Josephine Johnson, who went to her for a sign.

Josephine had recently undergone a successful kidney transplant in which her daughter was the donor. She prayed to Kateri and to the amazement of the Doctor, was ready to leave the hospital in a few days rather than the anticipated month. In gratitude, Josephine had made the decision to take a large group from her reservation to the Tekakwitha Conference in Spokane, Washington (1982). This task was an enormous financial undertaking and to raise the necessary funds, she spent months with her friends making and selling tamales. As the date for conference approached, two things were apparent:

1. The fund was woefully inadequate to meet the expenses for this trip.

2. Her health was dramatically deteriorating as her family observed.

Fearful that she would have a relapse from overworking, they cautioned her to stop activities. Beginning to feel that she had taken on the impossible, Josephine needed a sign from Kateri encouraging her to continue this gargantuan effort.

Papago has been changed to Tohono O'olam.

Rita, Josephine & Ruth A. Johnson

Following Mass one day, she prayed at Kateri's statue and received the incredible message. Kateri smiled a loving smile in response to Josephine's question, "Kateri, should I continue?" Josephine knew then that the trip would be a reality but she didn't know how Kateri would arrange for the remaining funds needed for there were only three weeks left.

A MIRACLE was necessary! Shortly thereafter, Josephine's sister-in-law visited from the reservation and the incredible miracle occurred. Unbelievably, while shopping at the local store, she purchased a lottery ticket, winning $25,000, out of which she gave Josephine the desperately needed funds to make the trip!

It was a great success for this was the *first* time these native Indians ever left their reservation....forty-six of them! The conference was tremendously enjoyed by all and for Josephine's great efforts at spreading the devotion of Kateri, she was the recipient of the Kateri Tekakwitha Award presented to her personally at Auriesville, New York, several years later!

Father "Joe" and Kateri

Father "Joe" McDonough, S.J.
St. Francis Xavier Church, Phoenix, Arizona

The Kateri shrine at St. Francis' Church in Phoenix, has been a source of great consolation to many people. A holy retired priest, Father Joseph McDonough, S.J. (the McCauley's first friend in Phoenix, 1965), known by all as Father "Joe" or "Grandpa Joe" to the little ones, was instrumental in helping with its fulfillment by contributing much of his Christmas money gifts to the fundraising. His great love for Kateri was nurtured by the many years he spent at his first Jesuit assignment at the Martyr's shrine in Midland, Ontario where the saintly Indian is honored among the Martyrs.

Father "Joe," the Irish priest from Galway, was loved by all and was a part of everyone's family at St. Francis. Allan had the joy of cutting Father's hair each month while being well entertained with stories of the Emerald Isle. Our home was his home, as Father came and went as he pleased, dropping in to say "hello," or swimming in our pool several times a week. Once, after a new alarm system was put in, Father Joe inadvertently brushed against the patio ivy, triggering the alarm system to blast its ominous siren all over the neighborhood, inviting a visit from suspecting police who found... a friend, the endearing smiling priest.

Father Joe could always be counted on for prayers, friendly chats or home Masses, one of which was offered honoring Kateri in gratitude for Josephine Johnson's successful kidney transplant. When Father Joe wasn't engaged in spiritual matters or home visitations, he was seen playing with children, hugging babies or planting roses.

As Kateri spent many hours adoring God in the Blessed Sacrament, Father Joe attended the Consecration of every Mass at St. Francis Church, as his retirement gift to God. It was a familiar scene to see Father after the noon Mass at the Kateri shrine blessing a sick or crippled person with Kateri's relic surrounded by a group of Kateri's praying friends.

As Kateri's apostolate was visiting the sick and dying, so too, was Father Joe's. He always seemed to be at the bedside of the critically ill, just at the right time. In the heat of the Arizona summer, one of his visitations led him to the bed of a terminally ill parishioner, who the week before had previously insisted that he should not return in such an intense heat wave, but he returned to her, despite the then record breaking weather. Sensing that her end was near, Father Joe administered the Sacrament of the sick. She experienced total peace following her reception of the Sacrament and died only minutes thereafter.

On July 14, 1986, Kateri's feast day, Father Joe came to our home for his casual swim. He informed us that he would be leaving for Midland, Ontario, the next day where he would say a prayer at Kateri's shrine for our family. He kissed us goodbye and little did we know it would be the last time we'd see him for God took him before he awoke for his 6:00 a.m. Mass. The following week, the swimming pool was permeated with the intoxicating aroma of roses. Father Joe was in Heaven with Kateri!

Ted De Grazia with his 'Lily'   *Ted De Grazia*

Kateri's Farewell to her Artist

At about the time Josephine Johnson was invoking Kateri's intercession in front of Ted De Grazia's statue, he was critically ill with cancer.

When Kateri was alive, like De Grazia, she was known far and wide, throughout the Turtle Nation for her exquisite artistry, especially beadwork, embroidery and weaving. Though her designs were perfection, she was first and foremost a perfector of souls. Her tools were prayer and penance for she spent many hours in prayer and went to extremes to suffer as Christ suffered for her own sins and those of her people. Before she died, she promised those around her that she would pray for them from Heaven; she then instructed her friends to continue to pray and make sacrifices for sinners. Kateri's great sacrifices on earth merited for souls great graces from Heaven.

Tekakwitha: Artist of Souls

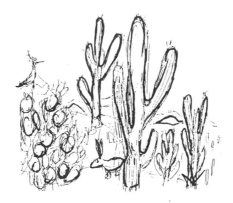

God blest De Grazia's soul, for he died in the loving embrace of Holy Mother Church, September, 1982. His daughter, Kathy, was happy to say that her dad grew to love the saintly Mohawk Indian who brought great consolation to him as well as being a major influence inspiring him to return to the Church before God took him.

Ted De Grazia's funeral was beautiful for he was buried at sunset in the earth of his desert sand. The following is an excerpt from a poem I wrote, after attending De Grazia's funeral!

"Lily of the Mohawks," bronze
Ted de Grazia
Photo: Dr. Felton Gamble, (Tucson, Arizona)

An Artist's Farewell (excerpt)

Seventeenth September,
Nineteen eighty-two,
His gallant fight over,
He bid his last adieu.

The sun cast a dazzling beam,
As mourners did trod,
On that Catalina scene,
Shuffling thru the sod.

Simple folk . . . the Yaqui clan,
Grasped tightly to the bar,
Of that which held their lifeless man,
So near and yet so far.

The white pine box, a loving task,
By Yaqui toiled-worn hands,
Below a cross, was set the cask,
In the heat of the desert sand.

A priest in vestments . . . black and white,
The service he began,
"Death is life . . . eternal light,
De Grazia . . . a great man!

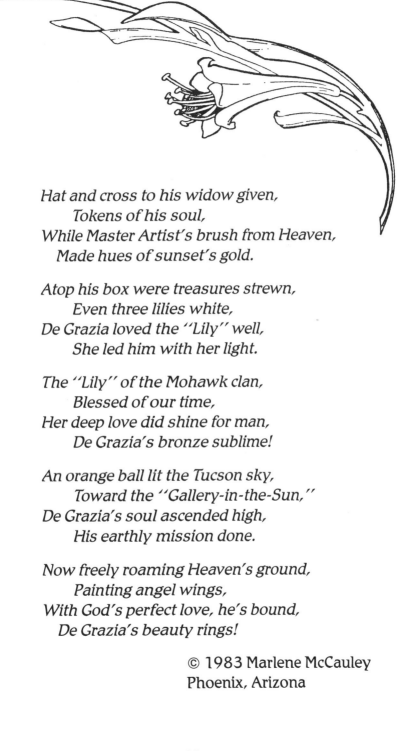

Hat and cross to his widow given,
   Tokens of his soul,
While Master Artist's brush from Heaven,
   Made hues of sunset's gold.

Atop his box were treasures strewn,
   Even three lilies white,
De Grazia loved the "Lily" well,
   She led him with her light.

The "Lily" of the Mohawk clan,
   Blessed of our time,
Her deep love did shine for man,
   De Grazia's bronze sublime!

An orange ball lit the Tucson sky,
   Toward the "Gallery-in-the-Sun,"
De Grazia's soul ascended high,
   His earthly mission done.

Now freely roaming Heaven's ground,
   Painting angel wings,
With God's perfect love, he's bound,
   De Grazia's beauty rings!

Fr. Ronald Schultz, Marlene & Hon. Robert Wagner
(former Mayor of N.Y.) at Kateri Reception, Rome, Italy.
June 20, 1980

Father Ronald Schultz, O.F.M., Conv.

We are lucky to have Father Ron Schultz, former Director of the Fonda Tekakwitha Shrine, (where Kateri was baptized, 1676, at St. Peter's Chapel), as he was gravely ill for several years, but thanks to Kateri's friends who invoked her intercession, he recovered.

During his illness, Father Ron's niece, Mary Himelrick, wrote: (Feb 1, 1982)

> "One night while Helen Wojnarowski was there with me, he had told us he had seen Kateri and the whole picture of her life came before his eyes. He remarked at the time, "She's putting everything together for me." (meaning, his health would be restored)"

> "Considering Father Ron's great work at the Fonda Shrine, over many, many years, it is only appropriate that we now have the recently constructed 'Rev. Ronald M. Schultz Memorial Building,' a fitting tribute to his love for Kateri and her native people."

Since Father's complete recovery, he has celebrated his "50th," visited Phoenix in 1987 for the Holy Father's visit (while staying with our family) and travelled to China on another occasion, his health still remaining stable.

Kateri's Baptism, Easter Sunday, 1676
St. Peter's Chapel, Fonda, N.Y.

Kateri Intercedes for Thérèse

During the beatification ceremony in Rome, our Holy Father commented on the similarities between Kateri's life and that of St. Thérèse, the "Little Flower."

Kateri and Thérèse both lost their mothers by death when they were only age four; both died in the prime of life at age twenty-four. Both shared the same child-like dependence on God, ever seeking to help the needy on earth, while retaining a beautiful simplicity of soul and great courage amidst much adversity and suffering.

The following story is about a friend named "Thérèse," after the "Little Flower," whom Kateri helped through an extremely serious illness.

Thérèse Ferre, the youngest of a family of twelve children was born and raised in Saskatchewan, Canada. Out of high school, she entered a convent but severe asthma forced her to leave.

Sometime later, her physician suggested she might try a warmer climate which brought her to Phoenix where her health improved to such an extent that she was able to perform as a nurse.

Thérèse's health continued to remain stable for many years until early one morning when she was found comatose by a neighbor. She was rushed to the hospital where she remained in a coma for forty-eight hours. She was diagnosed as suffering from an abscessed brain. During this period, Thérèse underwent intercranial surgery with poor response. While her condition was still grave, she was visited by our dear friend, Monsignor Neil McHugh, who blessed her with Kateri's relic. Almost immediately thereafter, she began to respond and ultimately made a complete recovery, attributing this to Kateri's intervention.

Thérèse prays in thanksgiving for her perfect health, each day at Mass, ever mindful of the day when God healed her through Kateri's intercession.

A New Opal

Why did an Indian friend, Opal Rector, give her Osage Indian burial blanket to the Kateri mission in Canada, April, 1991? She answered, "Kateri had helped me by putting my metastasized cancer in remission in 1985. Following this favor, I returned to the Church after having been away for many years!" She commented, "Though I am thankful for my greatly improved health, I am even more grateful that my faith has been restored and that I can once again receive Jesus in the Holy Eucharist!

In 1990, it appeared that the cancer had reactivated for Opal was to have surgery to remove two malignant tumors on the third and fourth vertebrae of her spine, followed by the insertion of a steel rod.

A group of us surrounded her bedside to pray the "Kateri Prayer" while she held the relic to her back. To the surgeon's amazement, there were *no* tumors when he examined her, just rock-like masses which he simply scraped off!

Opal has been spreading the Kateri devotion throughout her Osage reservation in Oklahoma and painting statues of Kateri, while all this time, her health inexplicably continues to improve.

Kateri Goes To Medjugorje

A pilgrim, Florence Ripley, diagnosed with a terminal blood disease, was about to cancel her trip to Medjugorje, Yugoslavia, where it is said that apparitions of the Blessed Virgin have been taking place for over ten years. Kateri was selected to be the Patroness for the trip. The spiritual guide, a Dominican priest blessed Florence with Kateri's relic several days before departure. That evening all her energy returned, enabling her to make the trip with eighty pilgrims! She returned from Medjugorje, symptom free! She too, has remained healthy to date and attributes her cure to Kateri's intervention.

Kateri Helps All

When Kateri moved to the Christian village where Indians of all tribes lived, following the gospel of Christ, she attended to the needs of the sick, poor and dying. She is ever-ready to help everybody!

The following is a story of how Kateri helped a friend.

Sophia Munson from Phoenix, came to our home shortly before our daughter's wedding in 1984 to decline the invitation because her husband Bob (a Mason) had just been diagnosed as having a terminal lung disease with very limited life expectancy, which precluded him from engaging in any and all physical activity.

Our dear mutual friend, Father Joe McDonough, S.J., blessed Bob with Kateri's relic and to everybody's amazement, Sophia and Bob were dancing at the wedding! Since then he has been praying an "Our Father," "Hail Mary," and three "Glory Be's" daily for Kateri's canonization—now, 1992, Bob is still alive!

"Death Is Life"

Fear not death,
    Death is soul's life –
Fear life –
    Life may be soul's death,
Smile,
    Pray,
        Love,
            Live,
                Give for God –
Close your eyes,
See your Creator,
Face to face –

Marlene McCauley
© Amityville, New York
~1958~

Kateri, Prayer and a Peaceful Death

Our sorrowful plight as humans, since the fall of man, has been to have to experience death. At some point in our lives, we all have to contemplate our own end here on earth. Whether we look upon death as a ghastly experience or an orderly transition from this life to the next, is a function of the depth of our faith.

That faith will be influenced in part by individuals who have impacted our lives by the manner in which they have responded to their own impending deaths.

One such person who made a tremendous impression on our family's acceptance of death was Dr. Dietrich von Hildebrand, (my husband studied Philosophy as a student of his dear devoted wife, Alice, affording us the privilege and great pleasure of becoming close friends of this extraordinary couple).

It was in the last ten years of Dietrich's life that we had become close to the Von Hildebrands, and it was at that time that ''Doc'' began to openly discourse on death!

Listening to Dietrich on virtually any subject, confirmed his great love of God and his boundless appreciation of the faith. Because our family was very devoted to Kateri, her name came up often in informal discussions. Crystal clear was the fact that ''Doc'' and Alice cherished everything this marvelous Indian maiden represented and considered her life to be a superb model for us all. For Kateri, death was looked upon as a reward from God for at last, she could be released from her earthly bindings and be one, face to face, with Jesus. Dietrich, felt the same for he wrote in his, *Jaws of Death: Gate of Heaven,* (Sophia Institute Press) written shortly before he died:

Drs. Dietrich and Alice "Lily" Von Hildebrand

"Death presents still a new countenance for those who loving Jesus with a profound and ultimate love, are consumed with longing for a face-to-face union with Him and with the Father, in and through Him."

Dietrich surely was one of those who loved Jesus "with a profound and ultimate love." The year before his death, our sixth and last child was born shortly after my forty-second birthday.

We asked Dietrich and Alice to be Godparents of Joseph Ignatius, the new family member. Both accepted without a moments hesitation, notwithstanding the fact that Dietrich was then eighty-six years old. He had often remarked that those in Heaven had great power to assist us on earth. We know that Dietrich was intending and did continue looking after Joseph's spiritual health after he went to Heaven.

Kateri, too, promised she would continue to look after her friends when she was with God. There is every reason to believe she has kept her promise. The signs that Kateri has great power in Heaven were apparent instantly following her death for her face became resplendently beautiful for all the pockmarks which had so disfigured her face, totally disappeared!

Our family has had multiple signs that Kateri is very much involved in continuing to assist her friends and one of the areas where the assist is most apparent is that of providing for a peaceful death. The reader will recall the account of Father Joe McDonough's death. Several other similar accounts follow.

Peaceful Death

Our son Peter's eighth grade teacher, Shirley Koscak, had her students invoke Kateri's intercession daily for her bed-ridden husband, a former violin maker confined for seven years with "Lou Gehrig's" disease. His joy was to gaze at a portrait of Kateri in front of his bed. Our dear Lord called Michael Koscak on Kateri's feast day, April 17, 1982. Seconds before he took his last breath, his countenance took on a peaceful glow and his dear wife announced, "Michael, it's the beginning of a brand, new day!" She knew he was with God and his precious Kateri. Since that time, Shirley became, Sister Michelle Edward of the Precious Blood, a member of a contemplative order.

Relieved From Suffering

How was my father exempted from all suffering from prostate and lung cancer before death? A priest blessed him with Kateri's relic and from then on, he was as peaceful as a dove. We asked Kateri to allow him to live for Christmas, (the day she received her first Holy Communion).

"Pop" enjoyed our family's carolling on Christmas eve and died two days later in God's loving embrace. He loved Kateri and had an endless list of people for whom he requested Kateri's intercession.

Kateri and the Holy Family

Kateri belonged to the Holy Family Association, an organization for pious members who strive for sanctity in their daily lives. The following story revolves around Kateri's love for the Holy Family and her special gift to a dying mother.

Sue Barger, a young mother of seven children from New Hampshire, in November, 1986 at the age of thirty-nine, was told by doctors that she was terminally ill with abdominal cancer. Her husband, John, publisher of Sophia Press Institute, (dedicated to publishing Catholic classics and reprinting the works of great authors like Dr. Dietrich von Hildebrand) coped with the horrendous ordeal heroically. Each night, he slept on the floor to be next to his wife; he did the cooking and cleaning for her and the children, devoting himself totally to keeping her comfortable.

Throughout the long experience of ineffectual medicines, operations and bleak medical reports, both of them trusted completely in God's Divine Providence.

After advising them to visit Kateri's tomb at St. Francis Xavier Mission, Kahnawake, Canada (Province of Quebec), the family of nine, made the trip in April, 1987. Though there was no physical cure, John reported that a deep inner spiritual healing took place.

Ten days before Sue died, she miraculously experienced being in the presence of the Holy Family and two angels. Though each day brought her closer to death, her joy increased. The night before she died, she assured John that the Holy Family and two angels had not left her. The following morning, she fell into semi-consciousness, drawing close to death. Her entire family, husband and seven little children, surrounded her bed, giving their precious mother a loving kiss goodbye. Each gentle touch to the mother's soft skin, evoked an affectionate response for she opened her eyes briefly and smiled weakly. Following the administering of the last rites of the Church, surrounded by her children with her hand clasped into his, she peacefully fell asleep, while the priest led them all in prayer, Sue went to heaven on July 17.

When Kateri was confined to her mat, and it was apparent to all that she was dying, members of the Holy Family association took turns at her bedside keeping her comfortable and praying, right to the moment she took her last breath, April 17, 1680.

Kateri certainly would not abandon this beautiful girl who made a four hundred mile trek, ravaged with agony and diminished by weakness. She, who could barely kneel at her tomb, was there with her entire family imploring with faith, help from this saintly Indian. Beyond any doubt Kateri heard her and answered her prayers. The Holy Family was Kateri's special gift to Sue Barger, assuring her that her family would be well taken care of. Several years later Sue sent John a new wife who has taken over magnificently. To this date, the family has increased to eleven and is managing beautifully and John has, once again, been able to devote full time promulgating truth for the greater glory of God.

Author's Note

The following background will provide the reader with an explanation as to how Kateri came into the lives of two people prior to their being burdened by a heavy cross.

When Cherri was in the process of conversion before her marriage to Katrino Gomez, the priest, Father Xavier Dietz exclaimed during one of her instructional sessions, "You remind me of Blessed Kateri." (Cherri has long black braids and looks Indian). When Cherri manifested curiosity about Kateri, Father referred her to the *Catholic Sunday Visitor* article, of June 22, 1980 which told about our son's hearing cure. After that article, when Cherri continued to show great interest in Kateri, Father Dietz, referred her to Father Francis Xavier Weiser's biography of her. Cherri, by now loving Kateri, decided to take her name as her own for confirmation.

Several years later, Cherri wrote:

> "God knew before we did that we were going to need a "special" friend to help us through the times ahead."

Sunshine for Life

The following is the story of baby Amanda Gomez, daughter of Cherri and Katrino Gomez, of Yoakum, Texas, born January 25, 1982 with a rare, very serious congenital intestinal defect, which prevented normal digestion of food. Shortly after birth, surgery was performed, which didn't help much. Soon, thereafter, Amanda was moved to the Children's Health Center at Galveston, where she lived with tubes inserted in her stomach and chest so that she could obtain nourishment. Amanda, soon became accustomed to the life sustaining machines, just considering them parts of her little body. For six months, the parents travelled 150 miles on weekends to be with their baby Mandy, after which time, Cherri decided to give up her job and to move in with her baby daughter, necessitating a separation from her husband Katrino during the week.

Cherri slept nights in an overstuffed chair to be at Mandy's cribside twenty-four hours a day, to keep the baby as comfortable as possible. Cherri learned how to operate the devices which kept her baby alive, thus eliminating the possibility of a delay when a timing device signalled the need for an adjustment of some sort.

Like his wife, Katrino, too, was incredibly devoted to his baby, for he drove from Yoakum, each Friday to be with his wife and infant daughter. When other parents with ill children complained that they couldn't take another day in the hospital, Cherri and Katrino answered, ''We couldn't take another day of being away from our baby.'' We are a family and a family we'll always be!''

Mandy was so incredibly endearing with her laughter and smiles, the doctors and nurses nicknamed her "Sunshine." How could these parents cope with such a hardship: separation from each other, a great decrease in earnings and the anxiety of not knowing whether the baby would survive.

"Baby Amanda 'Sunshine' Gomez"

Mother Cherri Kateri Gomez with baby Amanda "Sunshine"

The answer by these wonderful parents was:

> "We couldn't have done this without Kateri!
> From the day you sent Kateri's medal, it hung
> above Amanda's head, to remind us Kateri
> had a special watch over her. Many persons in
> the sixteen months that Mandy was hospital-
> ized, would ask about it and through it, we
> were able to tell many about Kateri, her life,
> her great virtues and her intercessory power."

> "Many of these individuals were moved to say
> an "Our Father" and a "Hail Mary," everyday
> for her canonization as we do. The medal helped
> us through those months and now it will be a
> constant reminder of Amanda, Kateri and God."

Kateri & Mother, Teaching Her Child Prayers

As time passed, the tremendous love and spirit of self-sacrifice of the parents for their little Sunshine continued. After many months of hospitalization, the baby was well enough to take a once per week five hour pass away from the hospital. During the first such pass, Sunshine was taken to Sacred Heart Church for a blessing and holy Mass. Mass became the routine with all passes, followed by other side trips to the zoo, beach or other places of interest.

As Kateri's mother, an Algonquin Christian, taught her prayers when she was a baby, so too, did Cherri pray with her "Sunshine" each evening. As they both folded their hands, they prayed:

> Now l lay me down to sleep,
>> l pray, Thee Lord, my soul to keep,
> If l should die before l wake,
>> l pray, Thee Lord, my soul to take.

Once when Cherri fell asleep from sheer exhaustion, (hadn't slept in two days), a sudden thrust of a tiny hand, startled her only to wake to find her little Sunshine with folded hands! From that time, never did Cherri forget prayers! The baby was then only nine months.

Not a day passed that the parents didn't thank God for their little "Sunshine." The greater the trials became, the greater they were drawn to God. When money was short, a check would arrive from fund raising groups of friends.

Slowly and steadily, over the next several months, to the astonishment of her Doctors, Sunshine's condition continued to improve, even to the extent that her discharge to home, was under serious consideration. She improved further until, May 17, 1982, when her condition took a drastic turn for the worse. Sunshine became feverish, lethargic and weak as all her systems gradually began shutting down. Katrino was called to come earlier than his usual time. The priest came to give Sunshine a special blessing as he and parents encircled the baby, intoning the "Our Father" as her condition worsened.

On May 18, knowing that Sunshine's death was imminent, the hospital staff, broke all rules; a rocking chair was brought to Mandy's room for Cherri. The baby, now in a deep sleep was wrapped in a blanket and placed in her mother's loving arms, where she slumbered her way to Heaven. What could be more fitting and loving for Mandy, than to go to sleep in her mother's arms, only to wake up in the arms of Jesus? The mother's beautiful account of the funeral follows:

> "It rained from the time she died and still was raining when we walked into Church for the funeral. I felt compelled to read a poem called "Sunshine" which described how God gives parents children, as a ray of sunshine and how these children are not promised permanently; God asks the parents to accept these children graciously and just as graciously return them back to God if He so asks."

"The priests walked down the aisle carrying Amanda's casket; next Katrino and I walked behind where we had previously walked before, on our wedding day. We both had an anxious, uncomfortable feeling."

"Just as we reached the big double doors at the back of the Church, the bells rang out real clear. The doors opened wide and we stepped out into the most brilliant sunshine we had ever seen. Katrino squeezed my hand so hard. I jumped and we both started crying and laughing at the same time. He said, 'Honey, look at that Sunshine ... it's for us ... SO special!!!' All the sadness was lifted from us from inside to out. Everyone said they were amazed after days of rain to see so much light and sunshine."

"We felt as if all the heavens and angels were crying for us here on earth for our loss of her. Even though we knew her spirit left her body and went straight to God, the moment she died in our arms ... still it was as if she rode a sunbeam right before our eyes to God, the moment those doors opened wide! The gates of Heaven couldn't have opened any wider than those doors of the Church. We were truly happy for Amanda and felt so good that God had given us this extra and special blessing to ease our feelings of grief."

A beautiful testimony for "life" was given by the niece of Cherri and Katrino at the funeral:

> "Every child born is a handiwork of God. God gave children to parents to love and help grow in the beauty of God's love. Amanda had a lifetime of love through her parents and she gave a lifetime of joy and happiness to her parents and to all. We love Amanda very much, her spirit lives with us all."

A relatively short time after Mandy's death, Cherri once again became pregnant. Being only human, she was very concerned about the health of her unborn child.

Soon thereafter, she received a totally reassuring message, for in a dream, she saw her baby Sunshine as an angel, softly treading through an endless field of roses, then stooping to pick up a lovely newborn baby girl and place her lovingly in her mother's arms. The sign was clear!

Mandy was in Heaven with Kateri and together, they declared the message that Cherri was carrying a beautiful healthy baby girl. Katie Moriah (named after Kateri) was born in perfect health, some few months later, to be followed by an also perfect baby sister, Gretchen Adriene.

Cherri and Katrino Gomez knew that Kateri had communicated to them that Mandy "Sunshine" was in Heaven. Like the Gomez family, all who have come to know Kateri, have developed a great devotion and deep appreciation of this lovely Indian maiden's profound and unconditional love for mankind. With this great love and intercessory power, Kateri never leaves a prayer unanswered!

"Our Lady of Perpetual Help"

"Kateri's Beloved Priests"
(Kateri's Galleria)

"My Priest Forever"

Faith, firm . . . . . real,
Burning zeal,
Love, warm . . . . steady,
Ever-ready to reap,
Souls to keep,
Eternally for Him,
Who in time's spell,
Will tell,
A song sublime,
Thou art mine,
My priest . .
Forever!

© Marlene McCauley
  Phoenix, Arizona
  January, 1992

Kateri's Beloved Priests
(Those already called by God)

Of the holy priesthood, Father Francis Xavier Weiser, wrote:

> "Receiving the Sacrament of Ordination, the chosen disciple becomes a living link in that unbroken chain of sacred ministry which carries the redemptive work of Christ from generation to generation....
>
> It completely envelops his being, so that his whole life must become a possession and instrument of the Lord's own priesthood."
>
> "Behold, I am with you all days, even to the end of the world." (Mt. 28:19.20)

The following five beloved priests who have been great promoters of Kateri, have one by one, been leaving this earth, accompanied by their saintly Indian to the throne of God. All who knew them will agree, that they have been loyal, obedient, holy and prayerful representatives of the Church.

Father Robert Fleig, S.J.
Oct. 15, 1986

Father Robert Fleig was one of those individuals, loved by one and all, who could always be counted upon to get the job done, unobtrusively, whether the assignment be large or small. Everyone who had the benefit of his contact, felt his warmth and understanding and were made better people, thereby.

Father Thomas Egan, whom he had worked with, at both the North American Martyrs' Shrine in Auriesville (where Kateri was born) and at St. Regis reservation, Akwesasne, Quebec, wrote:

"I wish you could have met even a few of the hundreds of people up at St. Regis, Akwesasne, who came to pay their respects at his wake. One person after another, characterized him as a kind, understanding, concerned, supportive man of peace, who lived the Beatitudes."

Father Egan added:

"A great tribute was given to Father Fleig by a non-Catholic writer of traditional Indian beliefs in the *Indian Times:*

'The Jesuit priest, Father Robert Fleig, S.J., was one of those rare individuals who left in his passing, a spirit of commitment, cooperation and compassion. He made an immediate highly favorable impression here. Our people found it hard not to respond to the warmth and genuine interest he showed for our community.' "

As a gift to his Native American friends, Father Fleig compiled a book, titled, *The Christian Indian's Prayer,* (the "Our Father"), which was translated into a variety of tribal tongues. This book was dedicated to his beloved Kateri.

Father Béchard wrote: "The Divine Master called to Himself, Father Fleig, Oct. 15, 1986. He was much loved by the Indians by reason of his great sense of humor and, for his devotion to them."

Rev. Francis Xavier Weiser, S.J.
Oct. 22, 1986

Though Father Weiser was a great scholar, having attained two Doctorates; one in Philosophy and one in Theology, he was a humble soul who was at all times ready to extend his religious counsel, consolation and advice to all.

For many years, Father Weiser was a Professor at Boston and Emmanuel Colleges, where I came under his spiritual influence. His greatest single contribution to us for which our family will forever be indebted was in the field of family life. In his writings and lectures, he strove to convey to parents, the importance of making the home, a "little kingdom of God," by the daily recitation of the family rosary as well as other spiritual practices, including: scriptural readings, God's altar, reading of the saints, Advent wreath (a custom which he revived in America), the pretzel custom, name-day celebrations and blessing of the family members. He demonstrated how his own mother made the faith more alive and joyful by practicing these liturgical customs in their home. His writings on this subject are beautifully compiled in his, *Handbook of Christian Feasts and Customs* (Harcourt, Brace & Co., N.Y., N.Y., 1958).

"Little Arms Crossed in Prayer"

It brings great joy to Allan & I to see our married daughter, Mary, continuing the beautiful seasonal traditions which we were able to inculcate into our family life, thanks to the dedication of Father Weiser for his apostolate as a missionary for families. How privileged are the newborns who receive the sacramental blessing of the cross on their foreheads, from their mother at the moment of birth and to have this practice continue throughout their lives as their parents continue to trace the sign of the cross on their foreheads as they leave the home each day.

Father Weiser's last beautiful memory of his mother was when he blessed her with the cross, just before departing from Austria for America, not realizing then, that God would take her shortly thereafter. Our last cherished memory of Father Weiser, was when Allan, Joseph and I visited him at Campion Hall, the Jesuit infirmary, shortly before he died. He admired the Indian dress I wore, saying that I looked like Kateri. When I asked him to give my rosary beads a little blessing, he laughed, exclaiming, "A blessing isn't like sausages that can be weighed....no such thing as a little or big blessing!" He blessed the beads and just before we departed, Father traced the cross on our foreheads.

Father Weiser's tremendous love and trust in Kateri's intercessory powers, was witnessed by his strong words that "Kateri leaves NO prayer unanswered.." The following is but one of many accounts of how Father Weiser's confidence in Kateri touched the lives of many, in this instance, that of a fellow Jesuit priest.

It was at Campion Hall, where he met Father Walter Abbot, S.J., another Biblical scholar, who was blind in one eye from falling down the Vatican stairs. Father Weiser introduced this priest to Kateri, having escorted him to Kateri's tomb in Canada. Though the Opthalmologist told Father Abbot that his eye damage was irreversible, Kateri, who had impaired vision on earth, interceded to God for him. A few months later, Father Abbot woke up one morning with 90% vision restored, totally convinced that Kateri had interceded in his behalf.

Father Weiser loved not only Kateri but her people as well. That this love was reciprocated is evidenced by his being invited to become an honorary member of the Mohawk turtle clan; shortly thereafter, he wrote to us about the colorful ceremony which took place during a Kateri weekend in Auriesville, at which time, he was photographed wearing the Mohawk headdress, which he dearly loved.

Father Weiser never told us his Mohawk name and because we could not locate it, my imagination created one....

"He-Who-Is-The-Weiser"

Following Father Weiser's death, Oct. 22, 1986, Father Béchard wrote, "Father Weiser was an extremely talented religious, who worked untiringly for the greater glory of God. Those who are close to the "Lily of the Mohawks," are particularly indebted to him for his excellent biography of Blessed Kateri. I will always treasure my memories of him."

Providentially, God took Fathers Weiser and Fleig within the octave of the feast of the North American Martyrs, as He did Father McBride, whose portrait will soon appear.

Father Michael Karhaienton Jacobs, S.J.
"Man-of-the-Woods"
September 8, 1987

Father Michael Jacobs, S.J., born to Anne and Joseph, was the youngest of seven children (three older sisters and brothers). From the time Anne Jacobs became pregnant she offered her baby to God. Sixteen years later during an outdoor procession, honoring Our Lady of the Assumption in his native parish of Kahnawake, Quebec, a thunderstorm forced the Pastor and his altar boys, one of whom was Michael Jacobs, into the Jacobs' home for refuge. During this visit, Mrs. Jacobs heard Our Lady say that her son would one day become a priest, a secret several years later, revealed to him, when he entered the Jesuit novitiate, on which day, she was totally cured from a chronic illness she had for many years. Father Michael Jacobs became the first Mohawk priest and ultimately was made Pastor of St. Regis parish.

Mary Cook, the only survivor of the Jacobs' family, resides at the St. Regis reservation at Akwesasne, (Quebec), with her husband, Dr. Solomon Cook, a Mohawk Chief. Two years after Father Jacobs' death, her daughter Michelle, (a Medical Doctor), was expecting her second baby after a first painful and unsuccessful pregnancy. An excerpt of a letter I received from Mary Cook follows:

> ''My daughter, Michelle, was expecting in February. She did not appear to be doing well and considering the loss of her first child before birth, we were all worried sick. Late in her pregnancy, she continued to have difficulties and was in constant severe pain. At this time, I blessed her with the Kateri relic that had been given by Father Béchard to Father Mike on his ''50th.'' The next morning, Michelle was dramatically improved, being almost totally pain free. She remained as such and a short time later, she delivered a beautiful healthy baby boy who was named Matthew Solomon Karhaienton (after Father Jacobs' middle name, ''Man-of-the-Woods'').

Relative to Father Jacobs' death, Father Béchard wrote:

> "Father Jacobs cooperated very faithfully with every Vice-Postulator since Father John Wynne's time in fostering the cause of beatification and canonization of Bl. Kateri Tekakwitha and was ever on the alert to communicate his love for her to all, a responsibility he considered his to the end of his life. On Sept. 8, Nativity of the Blessed Virgin, our only Iroquois Jesuit, Father Michael K. Jacobs, S.J., a truly admirable priest, was called to his reward."

Father Joseph McBride, S.J.
"Chief Beautiful Blue Skies"
October 23, 1988

Back in Auriesville, the land of Kateri's birth, dear Father McBride, ("Chief Beautiful Blue Skies,") while struggling with colon cancer, built a longhouse-style chapel overlooking the lush Mohawk valley, in honor of Kateri.

Like Kateri, Father McBride had a great devotion to the Holy Eucharist, which no doubt drew him closer to her and in like manner, gave him the strength to "carry on" through severe adversities. In the *Lily* of August, 1984, Father wrote:

> "Blessed Kateri loved the Holy Eucharist. Just below the stained glass representation of Blessed Kateri is the shining tabernacle. Looking at the window no one can miss recalling the connection of Kateri's devotion to the Lord in the great Sacrament."

Listening to Pope John Paul II at Angelus, St. Peter's Square
Fr. Joe McBride, S.J., Mary Eunice & Marlene

Needless to say, the joy of Father McBride's life as Vice-Postulator, was to witness his dear saintly Indian's beatification in Rome, in 1980.

Relative to Kateri's power as an intercessor, on the occasion of Father McBride's twenty years as Vice-Postulator of the Kateri cause in the United States, in 1987, he remarked:

> "The experiences of faith on the part of so many is indescribable. Personally, twice downed by sickness, prayers to Bl. Kateri by friends has me on my feet. What a privilege to be working for such a powerful intercessor as the saintly Indian maiden!"

It was said that Father McBride reiterated the following words about Kateri on many occasions:

> "She is the glory of the Mohawk race, a glory for the state of New York, a glory for all the United States and Canada and a glory for the entire Church."

Father Joseph McBride, S.J., died a year later on Oct. 23, 1988, within the octave of the feast of the North American Martyrs. He will be remembered for his great devotion to the Sacred Heart, The Blessed Virgin, the Holy Eucharist and Blessed Kateri who loved all three. His motto, "CARRY ON!!" will echo in the hearts of Kateri's friends for all time!

Father Ronald Sams, S.J., who assisted Father McBride at the Eucharistic Congress, wrote from Truk recently, where he is assigned working as a fund raiser for the Bishop:

> "I visited Father McBride's grave at Auriesville this past Summer and prayed for him. Now he is with Bl. Kateri interceding for us all!"

Father Joseph McBride, S.J.
Baptizing newborn Joseph
Old St. Joseph's Church, Philadelphia, Pa.
August 5, 1976

These words, *"Carry On"* rung loud and clear within our family's ears, especially when we had accepted Father Joe's invitation to perform our show at the Eucharistic Congress in Philadelphia on Aug. 3, 1976. Our baby's due date was July 4th so when Father Joe got the word that Joseph Ignatius was born July 31, he almost *fainted* when eight of us showed up at stage door on schedule, three days after the birth! "You just had a baby; what are you doing *here*?" We reminded him of his words, *"Carry On."* He became Joseph's spiritual Godfather, having baptized him during the celebration for Kateri at the Old St. Joseph's Church, a day after our show.

Marlene in role of "Meadow" (Kateri's mother)
Babe Joseph plays Babe Kateri (called "Sunshine")

Father Henri Béchard, S.J.
''Between-Two-Skies''
March 19, 1990

Father Henri Béchard, S.J.
"Between-Two-Skies"
March 19, 1990

Our dear Father Béchard, fell from his chair while watching the 7:00 p.m. news on March 19, the feast of St. Joseph (Patron of Canada). Relative to his passing from earth to Heaven, Mary Cook wrote:

> "Father Henri Béchard, our saint, left us so suddenly. I'm finding it so hard to accept. You know, I chose him to replace Father Michael, my brother, whom he knew and dearly loved."

Father Béchard, loved by all had the reputation of being a scholar par excellence on the life of Kateri and her companions. Father Louis Cyr, S.J., now Pastor of the mission of St. Francis Xavier in Kahnawake, (where the beloved Father Leon Lajoie, former Pastor still assists, though ill) spoke so eloquently of Father Béchard at his funeral Mass. An excerpt follows:

> "A gentleman to the core, kindness and goodness, his trademark... his coveted emblem and idea: a spotless and unblemished lily from the Turtle clan of the Mohawks, whose every footstep between the Mohawk and St. Lawrence Valleys became familiar to him. To whose blessed destiny he witnessed in numerous books, articles, congresses but especially in prayer and through his unshakeable belief in the sacred brotherhood of all peoples, native and immigrant, who have graced and enhanced the waters, forests, mountains and plains of both our neighborly lands."

The weekend of Father Béchard's funeral, dear Father Gerard Lavigne, S.J., escorted me on a trek following the trail of Father Béchard's daily life, beginning at the Church of the Immaculate Conception in Montreal where he offered his daily Mass for all of his Kateri friends to the tomb of his beloved Kateri, for whom he worked so zealously for over forty years. The biography he wrote of Blessed Kateri is presently being prepared for publication by the new Vice-Postulator, Father Jacques Bruyère, S.J.

Father Béchard was given the name,''Between-Two-Skies,'' (referring to his travelling to both the U.S.A. and Canada) a name which we now can interpret as meaning traversing between earth and Heaven, thereby affording him the opportunity for his continued promotion of his dear Kateri, even from above.

A Story of Doves

Once we owned three white doves: "Faith," "Hope" and "Charity." One day, "Charity," disappeared from its cage, never to return again. Several days later, when we were praying our family rosary, the intention was that we all have an increase of faith, hope and charity. Seven year old Joseph exclaimed, "But "Charity," flew away!" To that I answered, "Charity," our dove flew away to share its love with everyone and that's what God wants us to do with *our* charity; share it with everyone! The following is a story about another dove who flew away to share her love with all.

Princess White Dove

Princess White Dove

Princess Esther Kane Phillips, a Mohawk from Kahnawake, Canada, known as "Princess White Dove," was dearly loved and respected by all the aforementioned priests as well as by everyone who ever knew her, thus I place her in this section of "Kateri's Galleria," though the only woman and the only DOVE!

The former Pastor of St. Francis Xavier Mission, Kahnawake, Canada, Father Leon Lajoie, S.J. (ill health prevents him from working full time, however, he helps present Pastor, Father Louis Cyr, S.J.), commented at Esther's funeral Mass, "She was an institution on earth and I'm sure she is now building one in Heaven."

Princess White Dove possessed three outstanding gifts: a magnificent resonant alto voice, great artistry for beadwork like Kateri and a tremendous sense of humor. She was a member of the famous Mohawk choir which sang all over the world and whose voices could only be duplicated by angels.

Our family met her at the Eucharistic Congress in Philadelphia, in 1976, when the choir sang honoring Kateri. It was at the Congress, that we had a taste of her delightful humor. When a "paleface" approached her, inquiring, "Are you a REAL Indian?" She answered, "No, I'm a Japanese import!" Once when monologue actress, Mary-Eunice (Father McBride's assistant), was made an honorary member of the Mohawk clan, (with Fr. McBride), Father Jacobs and Princess White Dove gave her the name, "Princess Kasenniosta," meaning, "She-Who-Makes-The-Name-Of-Tekakwitha-Known-and-Loved." It was made quite clear (by the other Princess) . . . . "You might be a Princess, but you still have to do dishes!"

Princess White Dove had the honor of reading the petitions in her native tongue during the beatification ceremony in Rome, unprecedented in the history of the Vatican. Her deep, toneful voice, filled St. Peter's Basilica. A brief excerpt from my "Beatification" poem, follows:

"Let Christ's love be your leaven,"
Her beautiful voice reached Heaven!

This lovely white dove, disappeared from our midst on Nov. 6, 1987. She flew to Heaven to share her laughter, song and jokes with Blessed Kateri and her friends, leaving a trail of love behind!

Princess White Dove

*A Tribute to the loved ones of "Friends of Kateri"
who have been a great inspiration to us on earth and
have since joined the Church Triumphant,
we miss you! Please pray for us as we "Carry On" our
work for Kateri! The following list is only a small
cluster of the departed multitude.*

Rev. Robert Fleig, S.J.
Rev. Francis X. Weiser, S.J.
Rev. Michael K. Jacobs, S.J.
Rev. Joseph McBride, S.J.
Rev. Henri Bechard, S.J.
Rev. Joseph McDonough, S.J.
Sr. Mary Ignatius, I.J.C.
Sr. Winifred Scholates, O.F.M.
Sr. Teresa Collingwood
Sr. Marie Comeau, S.S.A.
Sr. Mary Felix, S.S.J.
Julia Egan
Betsy M. Egan
Alex Mitchell
Cecile Adams
Tom Constantino
Joseph Spagnola
Mr. and Mrs. Joseph O'Brien
Dr. Dietrich Von Hildebrand
Benjamin Monette
Lawrence Senten
Michael and Mary McCauley
Arthur Farley
Cecilia Letusky
Angelo Desideri
Sam Katsumato
Anne Jess
Edward Walker
Br. Raymond Bounds, S.J.

Harry and Margaret Stinson
Dr. Charles and Mary Steele
Sue Barger
Amanda "Sunshine" Gomez
Ted DeGrazia
Michael E. Koscak
Princess Esther Kane Phillips
Grace "Bea" Surrarrer
Kim Bailey
Red Bailey
Maria Garbarini
Mary Callary
Frederic M. Slavin
The Albert Matzes Family
Dolores Moreo
John McCauley
Robert Stears
Anna Mulcahy
Irene Rentz
Marjorie Leaf
Jeremiah and Katherine Collins
Barney B. Tesoriero
Katherine Beckwith
Mary E. Boley
Dr. Felton Gamble
Bill Healy
Mildred Herdrich
Anna Teplik
Martin, Peter & Darrell Burch

Interlude

The preceding accounts of how Kateri interceded for those who simply invoked her help are but a few from the McCauley family file.

If you wonder how our devotion to Kateri Tekakwitha began, just turn the page of time to "Early Days: Home to Rome," where you will understand how her seed of love was planted in our hearts, which continued to grow and blossom, spreading her magnificently sweet "Lily" fragrance of God's love and healing everywhere.

"From Early Days," our journey will be followed by a poetic account of the pilgrimage to Rome with Kateri and her friends.

PART II

"EARLY DAYS: HOME TO ROME"

Part ll
Early Days: Home to Rome

The year was 1976...The occasion was the International Eucharistic Congress at Philadelphia. Joseph lgnatius, our three week overdue heavenly gift was whisked away while but twenty-four hours old, cross country to perform in a puppet drama. Admittedly, such a 3,000 mile trip would be a practical absurdity for a newborn, but had he been born any later, the pragmatic "absurdity" would have been rendered a mathematical impossibility. As it was, the unlikely troupe of eight (six children and parents), arrived at stage door one hour before curtain time with the hundred plus piece puppet theatre, yet to be assembled. Somehow, the performance came off on schedule without mishap, with the newborn apparently relishing his role as "Babe Kateri." A day later the new addition was baptized by the late Vice-Postulator, Father Joseph McBride, S.J. at the Old St. Joseph's Church, after a Mass honoring Kateri. This was one of many cities in the U.S. we had travelled to, to perform, "Lily of the Mohawks," ever since our son Peter at age four was cured of a substantial hearing deficit in April 18, 1973.

It was our dear friend and spiritual advisor Father Francis Xavier Weiser, a Jesuit scholar and my former philosophy professor at Emmanuel College in Boston Mass., who while lecturing about his new book, *Kateri Tekakwitha* in 1973, suggested that we pray to Kateri for Peter, as, "She leaves NO prayer unanswered!" We prayed and prayed! Father Weiser left for Boston,Monday of Holy Week and on Holy Wednesday morning, April 18, (Kateri's feastday) we discovered that Peter could hear perfectly! Surgery cancelled ......hearing normal ever since!

Since Peter's cure, our family converted all energies into meaningful ways to make Kateri known and loved. Kateri was working overtime to help us, help her, help God! Hence, followed the development of the puppet-moppet play about Kateri and the creation of the 6' x 5' oil painting: Lily of the Mohawks "Kateri's Children of the World" — (cover illustration).

At about the same time, Father Weiser was lecturing about Kateri's extraordinary life and virtue, he also happened to mention an interesting bit of history relative to one of America's "unsung" staples...The omnipresent "pretzel!" Father Weiser explained that the early Christians during the fourth century had created the breads, as a lenten staple (they abstained from meat, dairy and pastry, a penitential sacrifice), shaping it the way they prayed, arms crossed over their chest, calling these breads, "Bracellae," meaning "little arms." The Monks of Northern Europe called it "bretzel," from which came the word "pretzel."

*Marlene in role of
"Meadow"
(Kateri's mother)*

*Babe Joseph
plays Babe Kateri
(called "Sunshine")*

*"Fr. Cornelius O'Mara holding a
Lenten Pretzel"*

*"Kateri Sings"
Anne McCauley*

Pretzels, Pretzels, Pretzels!
Left to right: Bob Westfall, Patrick Scanlon,
Ruth, Rita & Rosaline Johnson

Puppets, players, prayers . . . "PRETZELS" . . . why not? From thence sprung, "Pretzels for God." Kateri Tekakwitha was chosen as Patroness and within weeks, "PFG" was "off and running." God had been associated with many causes in the past but none quite as absurd as pretzel promotion! U.P. and A.P. picked it up and a deluge of radio station interviews, at all hours of the day and night followed. Shortly, thereafter, my husband Allan and I were invited to address the "National Pretzel Members" at their annual convention. Speaking to the giants of the industry on the religious significance of the pretzel at the McAfee, New Jersey PLAYBOY CLUB, was too incongruous an event to be overlooked by the ever vigilant eye of the press! The six foot painting of the "saint," "Kateri's Children of the World" was displayed on "centerfold" of the convention hall! There she was, model of prayer and penance at the Playboy Club! Soon after that, the *National Observer* ran a feature article with a giant sketch of the humble pretzel dominating center stage with the Patroness of "PFG" attaining national coverage!

With the "PFG" movement in high gear, pretzel bake sales at St. Francis Church were used for fund raising which led to a decision to use the profit for a shrine honoring Kateri! Who could be better equipped than Ted De Grazia, the artist of the Southwest to sculpt her statue for who knew and loved the Indians more? Ted needed to know who this holy Indian maiden was, for to KNOW her was to LOVE her.

A mutual friend, Brother Ray Bounds, S.J. was sent as an emissary to educate De Grazia about Kateri. He invited the artist to see our show "Lily of the Mohawks" which was being performed for the Yaqui Indians at that time in Tucson. The seed was planted but it was no easy task to get this goal accomplished, because the first response from De Grazia's "Gallery-in-the-Sun" in Tucson was negative.

"De Grazia is no longer doing any sculpting and is spending most of his time out of town" . . . . etc., etc.

It was time to call upon Kateri to help us, help her, help God! "HELP!" On an inspiration, shortly thereafter, a call was made to De Grazia who just happened to be home!

Me: "Hello Ted. I'm Marlene McCauley from St. Francis Church in Phoenix. Kateri Tekakwitha inspired me to call you."

He: "You hear voices too? She's been on the back of my mind."

I took a deep breath and in the calmest tone, . . .

Me: "Kateri wants you to sculpt a statue of her. You've been painting pictures of the Indians and she loves ALL tribes. She will one day be the first North American Indian Saint and will ask God's blessings for you if you help her cause!"

A short dialogue ensued about when we wished the statue to be finished — De Grazia seemed to be giving in but *not* completely.

He: *"We'll see.* Send me material every now and then to keep me "tuned-in to Kateri!"

Me: "Okay...by the way...what will it cost?"

(I learned years ago, that sale by presumption was the most effective approach)

He: "I will not charge a penny for my labor...The only cost will be in casting and I'll look around for the best price....."

Me: "Thank you De Grazia! You'll find that Kateri will be your best friend! She will help you in everything you do!"

He: "I need a friend like that!"

Me: "We'll raise whatever we need by selling PRETZELS ....you know, the little breads with arms crossed in prayer!"

He: "Set up a few barrels of "Bud," it will do wonders for the pretzel business!" (both belly laugh)

After many attempts at sending "tune-in" material, a period of three months passed with *no* assurance that Kateri was "en route!" The "saint" once again inspired me to call De Grazia one fine day, and as usual, he answered. A meeting was planned at his gallery in Phoenix for the following day, at which time, I found myself unfolding the story of Kateri to De Grazia, and Buck Saunders, the gallery owner. The artist seemed to be very receptive to the idea of sculpting the statue. Then, at the end of our session, De Grazia autographed his illustrated book *St. Francis of Assisi* at my request. He signed the book as I had seen him sign many such in the past. The meeting had gone extremely well and all was settled......I thought! The "Me" gave a BIG kiss on the "He's" grizzled cowboy's face and left "dancing on clouds!"

Once home I observed with shock, adjacent to the artist's signature, jutting out ominously, the phrase: "We Will See"

"We Will See"

De Grazia

1-27-78

Joseph the Pretzel Maker

Pretzel Baking is Fun
Mary McCauley & Kerry Lyons

WE WILL SEE
DE GRAZIA 1/27/78

Again, those words . . . . Those three little words continued to cause many sleepless nights! No meager effort was spent attempting to contort the language to conclude that "WE WILL SEE," and "IT WILL BE," were equivalents. Success in this pursuit of logical contradictions was not to be mine. Finally realizing that mental torture was getting NO where, I returned to De Grazia's original directive to keep him "tuned-in" to Kateri. The "tuning" notes were penned from points as remote as the "Emerald Isle" and as proximal as Tucson coffee shops!

Though there was NO activity from De Grazia, the homefront was teeming with life . . . PRETZELS . . . PRETZELS . . . soft, hard, candy-coated, pretzel cookies . . . pretzel donuts . . . pretzel bread . . . If any pastry or bread looked anything like a pretzel, we sold it to raise money for the statue!

A little over a year and a half went by since those MYSTERIOUS words "WE WILL SEE," and still no statue! The last resort . . . . a NUDGE NOTE!

July 7, 1979

Dear Ted:

Just a note to say "HI" from little Kateri and me. "HI!"

How LONELY is the space at St. Francis Xavier Church that awaits patiently, the "Lily!"

Enclosed is a Kateri key chain which will serve as a reminder that Kateri is LOVE and will open many doors, especially, the door to your heart!

(Enclosed "key chain")   Affectionately,
                                  Marlene

At the end of August, the moment came. It was after dinner when our family gathered for the rosary. The intention being that the statue would be ready for the 300th anniversary of Kateri's death (by the following April). When the rosary was finished, the head of the home announced:

> "Darling... forgot to tell you but De Grazia left word at the office two weeks ago that you were to call him! I was heading East to meet you guys and his message slipped my mind. If I'm not totally losing my less than tenancious grasp on reality... I believe, he said,

"THE STATUE WAS READY!!!"

Exuberant with the good news, I called to learn that "Kateri" was ready for inspection before her trip to the caster, to be immortalized in bronze! At this time, the artist advised that he was so pleased with Kateri that he decided to keep the first statue for his gallery and have the second one for St. Francis, from the same mold. He commented, "Since Kateri has been in my studio, she's brought much good luck!"

We fell instantly in love with little Kateri. Her slightly downcast face delicately suggesting an endearing modesty... her tiny hands softly caressing a pristine lily were a charming contrast to her rugged moccasins.... too large to provide more than the vaguest of support for the tiny feet encased, therein.....

Ted De Grazia was the recipient of the 1980 Kateri Tekakwitha Award from the National Kateri Center, Auriesville, N.Y. for his contribution to the cause of Venerable Kateri. All that was left to be done was planning for Kateri's 300th Anniversary celebration and to complete construction of her shrine.

The Mass and dedication on April 20, 1980 was magnificently beautiful! St. Francis's Church overflowed with ecstatic faces! The Native Americans beamed with pride as they sang and danced, giving tribute to their saintly Indian, Venerable Kateri Tekakwitha, commemorating the 300th anniversary of her death. They came from all over Arizona: Gila Bend, Covered Wells, Sells, Sacaton, Laveen, San Xavier, Santa Rosa and from as far away as Gallup, New Mexico.

Kateri's 300th Anniversary Celebration

A Merry Fiesta in the Sun
(St. Francis Xavier Church) Phoenix, Az.

Father Jim O'Brien, Vicar of the Indians of the Diocese of Phoenix, gave the readings in Papago while a Papago gave readings in English. The Mass music was especially written by the choir director Jean Robinson for this special occasion. A little Blackfoot, named "Kateri" made her first Holy Communion. In the front pew, sat a Navajo mother with her newborn in a cradleboard... coincidentally, she too was named "Kateri,"... our newest Godchild!

The dedication of the De Grazia statue by the late Bishop James Rausch was accompanied by "Miss Kateri of 1980," Ruth Anne Johnson, a Papago and Tina Leon, a little Pima, who presented bouquets of lilies. The bronze statue, "Lily of the Mohawks," in its classic beauty appeared suspended in air. The featureless face, radiating the self-effacing personality of Kateri Tekakwitha, who gave up her ego to be Christ-filled, seemed to smile! De Grazia had captured her essence, her sweet shy nature and a loving, humble simplicity. The gems in the feather accentuated her virtues while the turquoise stones in the base represented her joy at being welcomed to the Southwest!

At the end of the Mass, Bishop James Rausch announced:

> "Pope John Paul II has officially declared that Venerable Kateri Tekakwitha will be made "Blessed," the second stage to Sainthood....at a Beatification ceremony in Rome on June 22.

> "Tekakwitha" means "stumbling and bumping" into things or "feeling-one's way."

Our "saint" stumbled and bumped her way through adversity, finding God's precious light of truth. Therefore, her name can be interpreted as "she-who-puts-all-in-order!" She did! She does!

Ruth Ann Johnson & Tina Leon
at Dedication of De Grazia's statue of Kateri

Rita & Ruth

Kateri's 300th Anniversary Celebration

PART III

"KATERI AND FRIENDS AT ROMA"
POETIC ACCOUNT
OF THE
SEVEN DAY PILGRIMAGE TO ROME
JUNE 19 - JUNE 26
1980

To witness
a great moment in history
when an Iroquois virgin from
the Eastern woodland
of newborn America
received her crown
as "Blessed"

"An angel halted the March wind wild..."

Prologue

Good News

News of the Beatification of Ven. Kateri Tekakwitha
Reaches the Allan Mc Cauley Family
Phoenix, Arizona
March, 1980

An angel halted the March winds wild,
　　To announce the exalting of Heaven's child,
Maid of the woods...gentle and meek,
　　For Venerable Kateri...a beatific leap!
''Blessed,'' she'll be on earth's domain,
　　Honors of the altar,'' she'll attain!
All earth arisened from a long night's sleep,
　　The harvest of toil hers to reap!
The proclaimed news from East to West,
　　Reaching Mc Cauleys filled with zest!
Exhilaration at such a peak,
　　Young son Peter...first to speak,
''Oh, are we so satisfied,
　　KATERI SOON...BEATIFIED,''
Her soul...a lily without taint,
　　Now let's pray...next a Saint!''
All agreed...knelt side by side,
　　Though three hundred years since she died,
Felt her loving spirit there,
　　''Thank you God,'' began the prayer!
The Springtime desert seemed to know,
　　As the Western sunset cast a glow,
A lemon moon burst with smile,
　　As oranges danced from mile to mile,
The giant cactus seemed to say,
　　A happy end through a long, hard way!

Fr. Roger McAuliffe, S.J., Most Rev. Bishop James Rausch &
Fr. Edmond Smyth, S.J.
Procession at mass, for Kateri's 300th Anniversary &
Dedication of the Kateri statue.

St. Francis Xavier Church
Phoenix, Arizona
April 12, 1980

Phoenix rocked with elation,
    To hear of Kateri's beatification,
Timely for their celebration,
    Lend a dimension...a BIG sensation!
The sculptor's work, at last, complete,
    April 20th...the Bishop did meet,
For a Mass and dedication,
    Kateri "bronze"..."De Grazia's...creation!
St. Francis Church, packed to peak,
    Many could not find a seat,
Indians came from far and wide,
    To learn of Kateri...a great pride!
Ethereal voices filled the air,
    Chanting tones for the "Lily" fair,
The bell rang out for one and all,
    Time for treats in the hall!
A four foot cake for Kateri,
    T'was her anniversary!
Songs sung, dances done,
    A merry fiesta in the sun!

Four Foot Cake for Kateri's 300th Anniversary

Date Set: Can We Go?

A few days of rest...the wheels turned,
　　The official date we learned,
June 22...the beatification,
　　From the Vatican for edification!

A letter from the Vice-Postulator came,
　　In it, a Rome trip...did explain,
Bishop Hubbard of Albany,
　　Leader of the group, he'd be!

Arrangements made through "Triple M"
　　Limited seats..."Hurry, reserve them!"
The people would meet at "JFK,"
　　On the 19th of June...not far away!

Return on the 26th...the eighth day,
　　At the "Nord Nuova," the guests would stay,
"No chance of going," Allan did say,
　　"I'm swimming in 'gators' all the way!"

"The court calendar is a clutter,
　　I'm in a state of flutter,
Cases are popping, trials are set,
　　Still a house to be sold yet!"

"There are all types of litigation,
　　June is no time for vacation,
Don't pressure me to bend or sway,
　　Go without me, if you may!"

Went off to talk to God alone,
　　"If You will us to go to Rome,
Then You make everything just right,
　　Please nudge Allan with all Your MIGHT!"

The prayer answered in the middle of May,
    Order was made in every way,
Without the least hesitation,
    "YOU CAN MAKE THE RESERVATION!"

Soon the work with "Triple M" done,
    On time...limit, "eighty-one!"
The Mc Cauleys all rejoiced with glee,
    "Mom's prayer answered PERFECTLY!"

The older children...preparing for school,
    Summer learning, a great tool,
The two youngest were left to go,
    Peter, eleven and three year "Joe!"

Joseph played, "Babe Kateri,"
    Eucharistic Congress...day three,
Peter was favored with a hearing cure,
    By Kateri, on her feast at four!

Into high gear, departure at hand,
    Tried to stay calm through every demand,
The "to do" list...a mile long,
    So nothing could go wrong!

A suitcase each and a carry-on,
    Any space, soon gone,
Packed a gift for the Pope,
    With cardboard, paper and some rope.

Two hundred prints in a tube,
    A prayer thanking St. Jude!
"Oops, must make room for one more thing,
    A box of chocolates we must bring!"

New York Bound

Car in great shape all around,
 "GOODBYE PHOENIX...we're New York bound!"
Whizzed cross the states like a bird,
 To miss the plane would be absurd!

Arrived at "Big Apple" the day before,
 Had some sleep, then shopped some more,
Left for the airport in plenty of time,
 Traffic HEAVY, weather fine!

"A BACKWAY ROUTE!" Allan roared,
 "Soon it will be time to board!"
Made it by minutes five,
 Lucky to be still alive!

Found the agent mid the din,
 Got our tickets...heads did spin!
Threw the cases on the bin,
 Last minute scrambling is a sin!

Ran in and out and all about,
 Little Joseph began to pout,
Was here and there and everywhere,
 Had not a minute left to spare!

At last we joined the boarding line,
 "Thank You God,...made it on time!"
Greeted friends one and all,
 Waiting for Alitalia's call!

Happy to be of the "Red Button" band,
 Symbol of Kateri's loving hand!
Soon seated and calmly set,
 T'was 6:45 on the Boeing jet!

Fr. Robert Bogan, O.F.M., Conv. and Father Jim Rallahan S.J.

Sr. Dorothy, Marlene & Allan

Merry Pilgrims Take-Off!
New York: JFK Airport
June 19, 1980

The merry pilgrims were on their way,
    Like "81" flavors, so varied were they,
Most delightful group...ever met,
    From professionals to the homespun set!

T'was just like a melting pot,
    Of all races...where oneness wrought,
Some were single...some were not,
    All were a humble lot.

Brothers, sisters, husband-wife teams,
    Of all walks of life...seems,
From Auriesville and Fonda staffs,
    People sharing many laughs!

The Bishops of Rochester and Albany,
    The "Vice-Postulator" of Kateri,
"Father Mc Bride,"...so happy,
    Franciscans, Jesuits...other clergy!

"Little Peacock," of the Mohawk clan,
    "Iron Eyes Cody," a colorful man,
A Cherokee, in dress of tan,
    On TV...has many a fan!

"Mary-Eunice" of the monologue,
    Everyone engaged in dialogue,
"Peter," "tennis," with a Good Shepherd nun,
    "Sister Dorothy"...full of fun!

The Clouds are like Marshmellow Fluff

Joseph & Peter

Father Egan's mini-session,
    For Allan, an Italian lesson,
Told a joke at later time,
    Of mishap on "Alitalia" airline.

During the chatter of "this and that" stuff,
    Joseph finally loosened his cuff,
"Look, the clouds are MARSHMALLOW FLUFF!"
    "Some are like cotton puff!"

Photos snapped from the floor,
    Of happy people by the score,
A few dozing ones...then more,
    While the plane to Heaven...soar!

Dinner served, glad to eat,
    Roast beef...a delectable treat,
The bright red button did each one wear,
    "Kaiatonoran," her virtue rare!

Darkness drew its curtain bare,
    Now...a pilgrimage of prayer!
Silence hovered in the air,
    God's children in His care!

All these pilgrims dedication,
    To Rome for the beatification,
Giant bird...ONWARD RIDE,
    To your destiny glide!

"Airport Scene"

"Allan with Photographer Anne"

Arrival at Da Vinci Airport
Rome, Italy
June 20, 1980

After seven hours in Heaven,
    Arrived at Da Vinci...our leaven,
Got our luggage...wait, wait, wait,
    Custom clearing..."To the bus gate!"

Director of the Martyr's Shrine,
    Father Egan's face did shine,
Weighted with boxes and bags galore,
    Stopped to adjust before the door.

Carrying a cumbersome painting grand,
    A "beast of burden" in demand!
Or perhaps another hand?
    This priest ...in full command!

Didn't mind the stress and strain,
    A gift for the Pope...worth the pain!
Greeted by photographer, "Anne,"
    Father Mc Bride's helper from Kateri-land!

The Roman sky...robin-egg blue,
    Welcoming sun said, "How do you do!"
Whimsical waters at morning play,
    Dancing hues in crystal spray!

Majestic sculpture did abound,
    Magnificent art...so profound,
The old and new stood side by side,
    To St. Mary Major...the bus did ride!

Bus "64"

"Concelebration: St. Mary Majors"
Photo: Anne Scheureman

Mass at St. Mary Major

Eternal city of Christendom,
    Kateri's celebration we come!
Antonella and Machismo,
    Our friendly guides to and fro.

Taught us what we had to know,
    Of the Basilica...words did flow,
"Pope Liberius in a dream,
    The Queen of Heaven, he had seen!"

Snow will fall on an August day,
    Build a Church there...no delay,"
Its structure stands in majesty,
    The first to Mary...fifth century!

Ornate pillars...ceilings of gold,
    Our hands in fervent prayer fold,
A Mass in concelebration,
    Thanksgiving for beatification!

To the "Altar of Bethlehem's manger,"
    "Dear God, protect us from all danger,
For everything we thank you Lord,
    Please get us safely to the Nord!"

Through a discordant traffic race,
    Our bus rode at harmonious pace,
Arrived weak and weary...nearly dead,
    Hungry mouths to be fed!

Opened the chocolates...began to munch,
    Two pounds for Mc Cauley's lunch,
Soon there wasn't a stir or peep,
    Four bodies...FAST ASLEEP!!!

Marlene with Peter

Reception at the Grand Hotel
for the Kateri Group
Evening of June 20, 1980

Up from slumber feeling great,
　　Time to prepare for an evening date,
A reception at the Hotel Grand,
　　The finest one in Roman-land!

T'was the 20th of June...a Friday eve,
　　Soon it would be time to leave,
Showers, shaving...much to do,
　　Outfits chosen...red, white and blue!

Hurried, scurried as time did fly,
　　"Wear your turtle bola tie!"
There were many don'ts and do's,
　　"Must I wear my Sunday shoes?"

The silver cross around mom's neck,
　　Earrings matching...handsome set,
After all were in clean dress,
　　Joseph made quite a mess.

Chocolate over his angel face,
　　Soapy water did erase,
Boys were clean from toes to head,
　　Must not forget our badges, "RED!"

Father Joseph McBride, S.J., Terrence Cardinal Cooke,
Bishop Howard Hubbard, Msgr. Paul Lenz

A sumptuous feast served buffet...

"A Guilded Palace Hall"
Grand Hotel, Rome, 1980

All decked out in best array,
    Mc Cauleys soon were on their way,
The President of the U.S.A.
    A few days at the "Grand" would stay!

His bodyguards were everywhere,
    Felt we had them in our hair,
Could barely make it through the door,
    Then found them pacing on the floor!

Joseph cried, "It must be fun,
    To carry around a real, big gun!"
Ushered to the reception line,
    To meet the host and hostess..."fine!"

Honorable Wagner and Phyllis, his wife,
    Vatican ambassadors...busy life,
Planned this elegant reception,
    Will describe it...no deception!

A sumptuous feast served "buffet,"
    To walk around it would take a day,
On every table a rose bouquet,
    Tiny blue asters and baby breath spray!

A gilded palace hall it seemed,
    Everybody's faces beamed,
All who attended this fest so royal,
    Loved Kateri...to her were loyal!

Reception at the Hotel Grand
Photo: Anne Scheureman

Cardinal Terrence Cooke with Peter

John Cardinal Krol, Joseph and Marlene

To the chandelier...wished to fly,
    A colorful spectacle to spy,
Some were dressed in fuschia hues,
    Tones of reddish, purple, blues.

Cardinals: Cooke, Krol and Baum,
    Sharing as they strode along,
Talking, smiling to big and small,
    Their happiness filled the hall!

Tables decked in candlelight,
    Clergy wearing black and white,
People moving to and fro,
    Voices blending high and low.

Cameras clicking, "Hold that pose!"
    Joseph picking a pretty rose,
Indian people in native dress,
    Endearing soul..."God bless!"

After a bit of happy festing,
    Peter took a chair for resting,
Very fine talks for some duration,
    By clergy for "beatification!"

All enjoyed the presentation,
    Of Kateri...no simplification,
Finally bid all adieu,
    The moon fading...we were too!

123

St. Peter's Basilica, Rome, Italy

A Private Audience
with the Pope and President
June 21, 1980

A new morn promised great things ahead,
    Up refreshed, dressed and fed,
To lose a minute we did not dare,
    On the bus to St. Peter's Square!

T'was June 21...invited to see,
    His Holy Father and President "Jimmy!"
Informed of a time delay,
    The group found a place to stay.

For souvenirs...some went shopping,
    To the "horses"...Joe went hopping,
On a "buggy," he wished to ride,
    Peter...snapped with Father Mc Bride.

Father McBride with Peter and Joseph

Called to line up at "St. Anna's gate,"
    To discover more time to wait,
While standing in the radiant sun,
    To our surprise, met Billy Antone!

The Phoenix "Mass," the connection,
    Greeted him with great affection,
Dressed in a multi-colored vest,
    His sparkling eyes revealed a zest!

To meet in Rome for the beatification,
    Surpassed our wildest expectation,
He was chosen from a selection,
    To be the Papago's representation.

Marlene & Joseph with Billy Antone

While standing, chatting with Billy,
    There was so much for us to see,
One sweet image, we'll not forget,
    "Father Simon," whom we later met.

Holding as if he would never part,
    A carved wood "Kateri" close to his heart,
While involved in meditation,
    Someone took our reservation!

Soon everyone was fast ascending,
    Two hundred marble stairs blending,
Couldn't rest...couldn't tarry,
    Joseph screamed..."Daddy, CARRY!"

T'was quite a delightful fact,
    That no one suffered a heart attack,
Soon we read a welcoming sign,
    "Papal Quarters...Clementine!"

Thought we found our pot of gold,
    A "private" audience we were told,
Expectation reached a peak,
    To learn..."We exalted soon to be meek!"

No one really was to blame,
    Life has its unexpected game,
Jimmy Carter's arrival changed the plan,
    Extra invites for this "special" man!

Bodyguards again appeared,
    Taking much space as we feared,
Seminarians joined the fleet,
    Native Americans in a special suite!

A packed-full room...not a space,
    Hot and worn...took a place,
Standing, waiting...not one seat,
    Holding Joseph...not a treat!

Peter, missing, where could he be?
    Heart was heavy with this worry,
Our gift, our gift, what shall we do?
    How will it get to John Paul ll?

A poem-painting of Kateri,
    "Security" to us the third degree,
"An original? WHO ARE YOU???"
    Took it to see what he could do!

"Oh thank you, thank you, kindly man,
    He put it in care of the Mohawk clan!
Then suddenly we heard a voice,
    At last a reason to rejoice!

"Standing, waiting... not one seat"

"Allan, photo...while you can,
 It's HISTORY at the Vatican!"
"Sorry dear, t'would be in vain,
 To photograph a voice...INSANE!"

T'was not long when we realized,
 The sound...just mechanized!
Mr. President spoke of peace,
 That hunger and disease would cease.

"A common pilgrimage for us all,"
 Though hungry and about to fall,
Tried to stand proud and tall!
 A second voice filled the hall.

Of harmony, our Pope did speak,
 "A better humanity each one must seek!"
"Faith, hope and love erases pain!"
 From his study, the sound came.

At last came the awaited time,
 "THEY'RE HERE!"...each face did shine!
There was no platform elevation,
 Though couldn't see...felt jubilation!

Heard our dignitaries declare,
 Highest praise for Kateri rare!
Pronounced her name without a flaw,
 "Gad-e-lee...Deh-gah-quee-tah!"

President Carter did exclaim,
 About Kateri's difficult name
"Holy Father and I spent all night,
 Practicing to get it right!"

President Jimmy Carter and Pope John Paul II
Photo: Anne Scheureman

Of harmony, the Pope did speak

Allan sought a Seminarian tall,
    To take a photo was the call,
Joseph screamed, ''I CAN'T SEE!''
    A kind priest took him from me!

Joseph was the ''lucky'' one,
    Viewing from such height was fun!
Soon he fell fast asleep,
    Told to us by ''sleepy squeak!!''

The Indians made their presentation,
    Bearing gifts with expectation,
Each one to the Pope did talk,
    Our gift given by ''Little Peacock!''

Hands shaken...blessing given,
    ''Did Peter go to Heaven?''
The meeting ended...it was long,
    The Native Americans sang a song!

Viewing from such height is fun!

Then like magic before our eyes,
    Came Peter mid happy cries,
"The grandest thing happened you'll see,
    Pope John Paul blessed ME!"

"Many big arms over my head did go,
    To touch the Pope's hand so low,
To give it to me in the front row!"
    Happiness did overflow!

"His other hand placed on my head,
    I'll never wash it off," he said!
"Shook hands with President Carter, too,"
    Joy sparkled in his eyes so blue!

"This was a great moment rare,
    Monsignor Lenz led me there!"
An unexpected gift to win,
    Like Christ inviting his babes to Him!

A prayer in thanksgiving said then,
    Peace filled where fear had been,
Scripture's words in our hearts did burst,
    "The first shall be last...the last, first!"

*Peter... next in line
to be Blessed by Pope John Paul II*

FROM THE VATICAN.

SECRETARIAT OF STATE   September 29, 1980

No. 45915

Dear Mr. and Mrs. McCauley,

The Holy Father has directed me to acknowledge the message and gift which you and your children offered for his acceptance on the occasion of the beatification of Kateri Tekakwitha.

He appreciates the sentiments which you expressed, and he thanks you for the support of your prayers and for your solidarity in faith.

His Holiness assures you of his own prayers, invoking upon you and your children strength and joy in Christian living.

In the love of our Lord Jesus Christ he imparts his Apostolic Blessing.

Sincerely yours,

Msgr. G. B. Re
Assessor

Mr. and Mrs. Allan McCauley
6237 North 15th Street
Phoenix, AZ 85014

A 'Trattoria' for Lunch
June 21, 1980

Spirits soared to the sky,
    Only wished that we could fly!
Trying to cross a Roman street,
    Matched a tough Olympic feat!

Out to seek a place to eat,
    Treading on cobblestone street,
We soon did find a "trattoria,"
    Seemed each item...a thousand lira!

Sandwiches stacked in grand array,
    "I could eat all," Peter did say,
Cappuccino to coconut juice,
    Devoured like lions on the loose!

Eating "Roman"...a great deal of fun,
    Enjoying our fare in the Italian sun!
Relaxing on a comfortable seat,
    From standing all morn...a wonderful treat!

The table dressed in gingham best,
    Pretty flowers.."fancy fest!"
A fountain in view, made the scene,
    Staring at it, Joseph did scream...

"See, what the turtle is shooting out!!"
    "Its mouth looks like a water spout!"
Rome...a marriage of ancient and new,
    Of culture, art and sculpture too!

At every turn our eyes were caught,
    Such beauty and charm by seeing...taught,
To pay our bill...no easy chore,
    Since it almost reached the floor!

"I'm stuffed," yelled Joey..."can't even walk!"
    His eyes...closing...then his talk!
Homeward bound on bus "64,"
    Happy to see the hotel door!

Fountain of the Tortois-

"The Pilgrim's Song"
(First Dinner Together at the Hotel)
June 21, 1980

Line up merry pilgrims...join the parade,
 March to the dining hall...don't be afraid,
Tis the eve of the 22nd...you know what that means,
 The next is for Kateri...UNREAL it seems!
T'would be difficult to remember all,
 But will attempt a brief roll call!
Paul Thomas and Tom Constantino,
 Peter and Joseph...the little bambino!
Mary-Eunice and Father Mc Bride,
 Iron Eyes Cody...side by side,
Must not forget..."Little Peacock,"
 And several of the clan, "Mohawk,"
Sister Patricia and Anne Scheuerman,
 Mrs. Angel and Gertrude Flynn,
Irene Ryder and Sister Eschen,
 Senorita Moreau of Spain,
Eva Kwasny...another name!
 Fathers Rallahan, Bogan and Kern,
Father Egan's secretary, "Fern!"
 Father Schultz and his niece, "Mary,"
From Arizona...John Henry!
 Helen and her husband "Barney,"
A great man...(with a speck of "blarney,")
 Father "Pat" Iannotti,
(Far from being "haughty,")
 Where could "Father Fleig" be-a?
Eating at the Cur-i-a!

Helen & Jolly Barney Wojnarowski

Together we'll share the first dinner in Roma!

Father Baldus...Walter, his brother,
    Bishop Clark's charming mother,
Marlene and Allan of "Mc Cauley's team,"
    The "Busch" couple...Chuck and Irene,
Sister Dorothy...the smiling nun,
    "Excuse me, PLEASE pass a bun!"
Sister Mary Catherine Rich,
    Sister Mary Elizabeth,
And the partnership..."Wallace!"
    Mary Conley from Albany,
Helen Duell and Jeannie!
    Mc Convilles, Mc Carthy, Connors and Cook,
Afraid these names will fill a book!
    Melissa, Margaret, Rita and Diane,
Monsignor Glavin from Amsterdam!
    Christina, Gladys and Rosemary,
"Hurry, hurry...pass the tea!"
    Theresa, Miss Poodry and Loretta,
What setting could be better?
    Must not forget..."Miss Lundblad,"
Or we would be very sad!
    Mr. and Mrs. Hart and sweet Anna,
Name them all...you'll win a star!
    Who is that...and that and that?
Evelyn, Mrs. Choi and the Rev. Pratt!
    Mr. Milunski and Mr. Krenz,
O'Gradys...Eileen and Florence!
    There is the pair..."Terrance,"
Father Latus and his mother,
    Surely there's got to be another!
Schelsinger, Von Schelling and Eleanor,
    The list is so long..."OPEN THE DOOR!"
Fathers...Powers, Sheedy and Scharff,
    Let's end with a hearty laugh!
Hurry..."PLEASE MORE TEA,"
    Whoever is missing..."FORGIVE ME!"

Spaghetti the fare...a pungent aroma,
  Together we'll share the first dinner in Roma,
Tales to tell of the day's adventure,
  Of happiness, weariness...nothing to censure!
Pick up your glass...let's have a toast,
  To our humble Kateri, we can boast!
May God bless us with health and grace,
  That Kateri's sainthood, we'll soon embrace!
The hall vibrated with happy chatter,
  To be together was what did matter!
Food was served without delay,
  The waiter moving with the tray,
Joey reached over to help himself,
  "To say, PLEASE PASS, is manners, our elf!"
"But he may say NO...you can't have bread,"
  "That's why l used my arms instead!"
Jolly Barney at the next table,
  Taught Joseph a little fable,
When he learned the "tricky piece,"
  We thought that it would never cease!
Desert was served with some tea,
  "Have another cup, John Henry!"
This friend from Phoenix sat with us,
  Cuddled Joey when he made a fuss,
Thankful for the delicious fete,
  To the lounge went the fleet!

For a brief friendly discourse,
>Before bedtime...our recourse!
Allan in a conversation,
>About the bus transportation,
"It is an amazing situation,
>That no one asks renumeration,
Why at no cost, we could travel wide,
>Peter, Joey and my darling bride!"
"Now don't despair," said Father Kern,
>When the truth, you now will learn,
The box for coins is in the back,
>"Now you'll be on the right track!"

Mama Marlene & Joseph riding bus 64

"Iron Eyes Cody" was very emphatic,
    About his camera...instamatic,
"No courage had I to "photo" the Pope,
    Standing so close, there would be hope!
With "Felici" and "Mari"...Vatican folk,
    I felt that I would be a joke!"
"With all my heart, I wished to click,
    Wishing and wishing made me sick!"
The eve ended with the final talk,
    "Report in the morn at eight o'clock!"
Last words given by Father Mc Bride,
    "Tomorrow we'll take our memorable ride!"
We bid "goodnight" for the day was done,
    Anxious for the morning sun!

"Iron Eyes Cody was very emphatic!"
Tom Constantino, Iron Eyes & Fr. Tom Egan, S.J.

The Beatification of Kateri Tekakwitha

St. Peter's Basilica
Rome, Italy
Pope John Paul II
June 22, 1980

Oldest Portrait of Kateri by
her spiritual director, Fr. Claude Chaucétiere, S.J.
1682-83

The Beatification of Kateri Tekakwitha
St. Peter's Basilica
Rome, Italy
Pope John Paul II
June 22, 1980

Heaven's bells pealed a tune,
    On the twenty-second day of June,
Of a nineteen-eighty glowing moon,
    To exalt a humble maiden soon!

T'was three hundred years this soul took flight,
    To be born of eternal light,
Her promise, "I will pray for you,"
    Heeded to many the centuries through.

Generations twelve, prayed for this day,
    Marked by God's providential ray,
The sun delivered a golden beam,
    Kateri elevated...was it a dream?"

Peter in Front of Vatican

Native Americans

Exultant hearts did overflow,
    Toward Mother Church their steps did go,
Native Americans resplendently dressed,
    To see their sister at last made ''Blest!''

Swiss guards at St. Peter's door,
    Meeting people by the score,
Standing stately, sword in hand,
    Pilgrims passing from every land.

Twenty-five thousand flocked to see,
    An outstanding moment in history,
To each a missal...then a seat,
    The Kateri group, left transcept did meet.

''Swiss Guards''
Photo: Allan McCauley

Lived within a hundred fifty years,
    Filled with faith, they had no fears.
Each accepted Christ's invitation,
    Peter Betancur to Marie of the Incarnation.

In their souls His grace did fill
    Joseph Ancieta..."Apostle of Brazil,"
Bishop Laval...the "First" of Quebec,
    Kateri Tekakwitha...of the Mohawk "sect."

Heroic virtue...their call,
    Proclaiming Christ's gospel to all,
In distant lands and Indian soil,
    Midst suffering, they did toil!

Americans and Guatemalans,
    Canadians and Brazilians,
Assembled for the Beatification,
    A Pontifical celebration!

"Beatification of Kateri Tekakwitha"
Photo: Anne Scheureman

From every where…all came to see,
 Five "Venerables"…made "Beati"
Two sons of Spain…two of France,
 All of missionary stance.

St. Peter's Basilica…awe-inspiring,
 Spaciousness…wreathed columns spiraling,
Canopied altar…golden throne,
 Above which soars Michaelangelo's dome.

Imposing edifice…Christendom's rock,
 Crypt of St. Peter…under this spot,
Antiquity-rooted…apostolic succession,
 Introducing the solemn procession!

Beatification Ceremony of Kateri Tekakwitha
St. Peter's Basilica, Rome, Italy, 1980

One of the concelebrants of the day,
    Jesuit General...Pedro Arrupé,
Bishops, "Arch,"...Cardinals, too,
    Took their places on cue.

Wearing red and violet zuchetti,
    Soon they knew the moment ready!
Lights went on...the organ resounded,
    Pope John Paul ll...to the altar mounted.

An endearing soul, filled with love,
    Missionary spirit, Poland's dove,
Christ's vicar, the Spirit's prize,
    Pope John Paul ll...with "Talking eyes!"

T'was an impressive, stirring sight,
    At the Penitential rite,
When the members did arrive,
    To petition their candidates five.

Silence reigned...Bishop Hubbard's talk,
    "Please count as 'Blessed,' Kateri, a Mohawk!"
Hearts beat in anticipation,
    For the Holy Father's declaration.

In robes of glimmering white and gold,
    The silver staff, his hand did hold,
Just before the Gloria rite,
    Announcement made from the altar's height.

Bishop Howard Hubbard & Pope John Paul II
at Kateri's beatification

Beatification Ceremony
St. Peter's Basilica
Rome, Italy
June 22, 1980

''By apostolic authority,
    Declare that Venerable Kateri,
Will henceforth be called, 'Blest,' ''
    Her life a miracle, severe the test!

''April seventeenth, the feast,''
    The day her heartbeat ever ceased,
A thunderous applause echoed through,
    Hearty clapping only grew!

Leading to a might roar,
    Vibrating the massive ''holy door!''
Tears welled in many eyes,
    Ecstasy, hard to disguise!

Indian people burst with pride,
    To see their own beatified!
Hearts cried in exultation,
    On this day of jubilation!

Blessed Kateri...God's love she'll bind,
    Gifts from Him for you she'll find,
'irtues jewels for emulating,
    God-filled ''Lily'' self effacing!

The Holy See has approved this Mass prayer which may be used on the Feast of Blessed Kateri Tekakwitha:

Lord God, you called the virgin, Blessed Kateri Tekakwitha, to shine among the Indian people as an example of innocence of life. Through her intercession, may all peoples of every tribe, tongue, and nation, having been gathered into your Church, proclaim your greatness in one song of praise. We ask this through our Lord Jesus Christ, Your Son, who lives and reigns with you and the Holy Spirit one God, for ever and ever.

The Sistine choir...Gregorian sang,
    In Latin phrases their voices rang!
"Missa de Angelis"...ethereal cadence,
    Heavenly tones...mystical radiance!

A Seminarian from Albany,
    Gave the reading splendidly,
"Your love and works are your worth,
    You are the salt of the earth!"

"Princess White Dove" from Caughnawaga*,
    An Iroquois mission in Canada,
Spoke the petition in Mohawk tongue,
    Her chanting tones strongly rung!

"Let Christ's love be your leaven!"
    Her beautiful voice reached Heaven!
For St. Peter's...an innovation,
    In native dialect...this recitation!

Our Holy Father's homily,
    Ending with our Kateri,
Praised her faith to God above,
    His sacred cross...her deepest love.

"Through suffering, she did impart,
    Resignation and joyful heart!"
"Last words as she bid adieu,"
    "Jesus, Mary...I love You!"

*Caughnawagha has been changed to the
correct Mohawk spelling, Kahnawake.*

Presentation of gifts...a spectacular sight,
    Indians dressed in regalia bright,
From United States and Canada,
    In line...approached the altar.

Father Béchard and Joseph Mc Bride,
    Observing this filled with pride,
Vice-Postulators for Kateri,
    And the General...Father Molinari!

Father Ron Schultz of Fonda Shrine,
    Overflowed with love sublime,
Father Tom Egan of Martyr's home,
    Pondered Kateri's path to Rome.

Director of "Missions,"...Monsignor Lenz,
    Happily watched his many friends,
Arrayed in full ceremonial dress,
    Beads and buckskins to feathered headdress!

Fathers Thomas Egan, S.J. and Henri Béchard, S.J.
Photo: Allan McCauley

"He-Who-Consoles-The-Mind"   *with "Between-Two-Skies"*
(Father Thomas F. Egan, S.J.)   (Father Henri Béchard, S.J.)

Native Americans burst with pride"

Potawatomi and Saketon,
    To countless tribes, they did belong,
Cherokee, Choctaw and Papago,
    Blackfoot, Laguna and Navajo!

The Sioux, Tewa and Mohawk,
    Deafening applause as each did walk!
Ben Black Bear and Chief Delisle,
    An entourage through the aisle.

Francis Hairy Chin and Iron Eyes,
    Cameras clicking to immortalize!
Big Chief Jim Shot Both Sides,
    Expressing homage of the tribes.

"To the great Holy White Father," he read,
    Presenting a jeweled band for the head!
Hopi pottery...in sienna and white,
    Kachina dolls...a colorful sight!

Papago baskets and a peace pipe,
 A Navajo rug with a bright stripe,
Jewelry made of brilliant seeds,
 Wampum belts of vivid beads!

With no concern for protocol,
 The Holy Father talked to all!
Little Peacock, gave a stole,
 "See the 'Lily,'...Kateri's symbol!"

"Look the turtle, wolf and bear!"
 "Thank you for Beatifying...Kateri fair!"
Pope John ll, blessed her there,
 For all...a memorable affair!

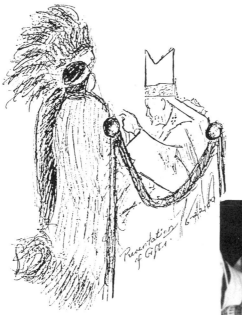

Presentation of Gifts
Little Peacock's Stole: Gift to Holy Father

Little Peacock

A beautiful Mass...the morning long,
    The entire Basilica broke in song,
"Holy God, we praise Thy name,"
    Blessed Kateri forever reign!

After the Mass, the Pope did greet,
    Each representative gathered to meet,
In the chapel of St. Sebastian,
    Spirit and love-light never dim!

The blessings complete...he left his seat,
    A message of love from the papal suite,
The Angelus bells ore Rome were heard,
    "Be it done unto me...Thy holy word!"

From the Basilica to the square,
    Pope John Paul's words...filled the air,
An afterglow...on each one's face,
    Knowing that Kateri, he did embrace.

In parting the Holy Father did bless,
    The Indians of Canada and the U.S.
Oh, Blessed Kateri...for all mankind,
    A sweet bouquet for earth you'll find!

Dear Mohawk "Lily,"...beyond compare,
    Fill us with your fragrant prayer,
Unite us in God's brilliant light,
    Let us strive to your great height.

Blessed Kateri Tekakwitha,
    God's effervescent star,
Humble maiden...free of mar,
    Your sainthood shines not afar!

Reflections After Beatification:
A Pleasant Surprise

A shock was ours when we did spy,
    Son Peter's photo before our eye,
The *Sunday Visitor* of June twenty-two,
    Held by a pilgrim in close view,

We were interviewed in Phoenix many months past,
    Now we discover; t'was printed at last,
We laughed with delight at this surprise,
    A front page article...before our eyes!

The lady wondered why we did peer,
    Explained we, "That's Peter our son so dear!"
"Take it!" she cried, from me a prize!"
    Such irony...who could surmise?

The writer reported all details to know,
    Of son's hearing loss cure and our Kateri show,
Will God's humor ever cease?
    Six thousand miles to read this piece!

Peter's eyes fixed intently,
    Happiness rooted, sat contently,
Kateri on his eager mind,
    "My little friend is for mankind!"

At the base of a niche...sculptured relief,
    Were marbled cherubs beyond belief,
Without the least bit of feign,
    "SEE THE ANGELS," Joe did exclaim!

Joseph burst with exclamation,
    "We saw Kateri's BEETIF-CATION!"
A difficult word for his tongue to say,
    Kateri smiled at his innocent way!

Joy blended on this special day,
    With Jesuit..."Father Bazinet,"
Fathers "Sal," and "Fleig" shared too,
    Cherished moments...RARE few!

Sharing binoculars so we all could see,
    Pope John Paul's smile...so close it be!
The "seventeenth" row so near the throne,
    Soon became..."Home Sweet Home!"

Feature

Peter thanks Kateri Tekak

By Margaret and Walter Regnier

PHOENIX, AZ — June 22 will be a special day for a boy named Peter McCauley. Peter will be in Rome with his parents attending beatification ceremonies for Kateri Tekakwitha in St. Peter's Basilica.

Peter, now age 11, was miraculously cured of deafness following family prayers on his behalf.

Peter was partially deaf in both ears. He could hear only the loudest shouts. One day a special friend visited the McCauley family in their Phoenix home. The visitor, a Jesuit — Father Francis X. Weiser — had knelt at the altar with Allan and Marlene McCauley on their wedding day years before.

Learning of Peter's deafness, Father Weiser suggested the family pray to Venerable Kateri Tekakwitha that God might graciously grant a cure to young Peter.

The family acted on Father's suggestion. One morning in Holy Week on the feast of Kateri's baptism — the last day of the family's novena of prayers — Peter's father whispered something to Marlene. And Peter answered. He had heard a whisper! The family was stunned. Then tears and prayers of joy and gratitude poured out. It was a never-to-be-forgotten moment in their lives.

Peter was four years old when he suddenly received his hearing. Medical records of Peter's "unexplained cure" were sent to Rome. Results of follow-up examinations by a team of doctors also were sent periodically to the Vatican. Thus Peter's case became part of the vast amount of evidence the Church collects prior to beatification and canonization.

McCauley family members share a warm devotion for their Indian friend in heaven. Shortly after receiving his hearing Peter and his family visited Kateri's shrine in upper New York State. As soon as Peter

Peter McCauley, right, with his mother, M now hears through Kateri's intercession.

saw the life-like statue of the Indian maid, he rushed up and flung his arms around her and hugged her. Every year since regaining his hearing Peter faithfully has sent his "Lenten denial money" to help Kateri's cause. He prays daily for her canonization.

Peter now has had seven years of perfect hearing in both ears. "He has never had a recurrence of any trouble," says his mother, Marlene McCauley.

Peter has three brothers and two sisters. His father is an attorney. His mother, an artist, has a college degree in theater

witha for miracle of sound

arlene, and her painting. They believe Peter
— Regnier photo

arts and crafts. She is the local director of
the canonization cause for Kateri
Tekakwitha.

The McCauleys are well-known in the
Phoenix area for their puppet shows and
skits. After Peter's cure the family col-
laborated on a pageant of Kateri's life —
"The Lily of the Mohawks." They have
presented the drama in many parts of the
country, including a performance at the
1976 International Eucharistic Congress in
Philadelphia.

"We wanted to tell everyone about
Kateri," says Marlene, who researched and
wrote the play. "Our aim is to spread the
love of Kateri. We especially want our
Indian people to know about Kateri. She is
one of their own. Young people need mod-
els, and Kateri is one of the finest."

The pageant portrays the life of Kateri,
her conversion to the Catholic faith and her
saintly death. In the drama the McCauley
Family Players take all the parts. Peter
plays the role of one of the Jesuit missionaries, Father Pierron. At the play's
end, Peter steps front and center stage to
present the cast and production crew.
Dressed as a "Jesuit Black Robe" his
child's face is dwarfed by a broad-brimmed
cleric's hat. He bows and begins, "By now
you probably know that I'm not *really*
Father Pierron. . . ."

An oil painting by Marlene McCauley
shows Kateri Tekakwitha within the company of children of many races. A likeness
of Peter is painted into the picture. The
huge five- by six-foot canvas now hangs in
San Juan Capistano in California in the
permanent art collection of the mission
church.

In April of this year, to mark the 300th
anniversary of the death of Venerable
Kateri, Ted DeGrazia sculpted a jeweled
statue of The Lily of the Mohawks. The
sculptor, along with Friends of Kateri,
presented the statue to St. Francis Xavier
Church in Phoenix.

Amid the flurry of getting ready to
leave for Rome, Marlene confided: "When
we received the letter inviting us to Rome
to attend the beatification ceremonies for
Kateri, I was so excited! But I didn't want
to pressure Allan about our being able to
attend. Instead, in my prayers I asked God
to pressure Allan. Then one day Allan said,
'Well, I guess we can go to Rome.' Our
plane reservations were confirmed just
before the deadline."

"See the Angels!"

*"Marlene, Allan & Joseph
with Fr. Sal Pantano, O.F.M., Conv.
during Beatification"*

163

Exploring the Vatican
(after Beatification)
June 22, 1980

After lunch, t'was Peter's plan,
    To explore the Vatican,
There were endless things to see,
    Dating to many a past century.

Constantine to Cavallini,
    Michaelangelo and Bernini,
Giotto and Maderno,
    Reni and Raffaello!

Crypt of St. Pius X,
    The Saint who went to great length,
Admitting children to Communion,
    The gift of Christ's union!

The Chapel of the Presentation,
    Next we saw, Transfiguration,
Then the Blessed Sacrament,
    These chapels from Heaven sent!

Viewed St. Peter's Crucifixion,
    Masterpiece defies description,
Archangel Michael by Reni,
    Executed with artistry.

The ''Pieta,'' and ''St. Peter's Chair,''
 Canopy and crucifix rare,
Venetian alabaster glass,
 The ''Holy Spirit''...glowing mass!

Baroque and Renaissance combined,
 Lasting beauty for mankind!
Prophetic words at the base of the dome,
 Soaring to our eternal home...

''Upon this rock, My Church you will build,''
 To St. Peter, spirit-filled,
Here on earth...a kingdom Divine,
 Promised to last to the end of time!

Piéta

Rome from the Dome

Winding steps we did ascend,
    Round and round...t'would never end,
Joseph, leader all the way,
    "We're flying to Heaven HOORAY, HOORAY!"

Soon we were on top of the dome,
    Overlooking the city of Rome!
Like a painting on display,
    Impressionistic...color-play!

Spent all day under sky of blue,
    A panorama of Roma's view,
The brilliant sun cast a golden beam,
    On the Papal Gardens...exquisite scene!

The key shaped piazza to the colonnade,
    Fountains, Bernini and Maderno made,
Wonderful place to take a seat,
    Before Reconciliation Street!

Crowned cross...touching sky,
    On top of obelisk towering high!
Trastevere...where Roman's meet,
    In the cold or in the heat!

Tomb of the Unknown Soldier
"The Wedding Cake"

St. Peter's Dome

166

The Tiber river winding its way,
 "See, a SNAKE," Joseph did say!
Another glance we did make,
 At Victor Emmanuel's "Wedding Cake!"

Famous "Unknown Soldier's Tomb,"
 T'was a clear view, this day in June!
Via Veneto for a shopping spree,
 There was so much to see!

The popular Villa Medici,
 The French Art Academy,
There's the Villa Borghese,
 The GRANDEST park in Romany!

Rome from the Dome

The Circus Maximus for chariot races,
    Roman Forum for Tribunal cases,
"See the Arch of Constantine,
    In history books, we have seen!"

Beyond is the Palantine Hill,
    Near the Colosseum where lions did kill,
The early Christians who died for Him,
    Who gave His life to redeem man's sin!

Example for martyr's blood,
    From whence did bloom a sacred bud,
Fragile and pockmarked...partially blind,
    Kateri Tekakwitha...for mankind.

While pondering on this lily bloom,
    Noticed the day had passed too soon,
The sun setting in the West,
    Time to gather our little nest!

The Lost Lamb...Peter!
After a Day at St. Peter's Basilica,
June 22, 1980
7:00 p.m.

Peter was lost, no where to be found,
    Searched the Vatican upside down,
"Knowing Peter, he's homeward bound,"
    His father's toneful voice did sound!

"Let's go on bus "64,"
    We'll see our son at the hotel door!"
Soon the three were on their way,
    Back to the Nord without delay!

Expected to find the long lost son,
    Engaged in play, having fun!
Not in the lounge or on the stair,
    Or in the room...oh where, NO WHERE???

Allan flew like a lark,
    Before the curtain call was dark,
Onto a bus, he did dart,
    To the Vatican in a spark!

A dear sweet nun, Sister Mary,
    A day at St. Peter's make her weary,
Searched every niche, nook and pew,
    For her friend who was lost too!

"During that time, there could not be,
    Anyone there...t'was EMPTY!"
Spirits sank to the floor,
    "Is Peter gone forevermore?"

One of the women did say,
    "My son at twelve, did run away,
Don't be worried, fretful, blue,
    My son came back, yours will too!"

Father Egan of Peter's return,
    "Someone will help with his journ,
He has a special friend, you see,
    Her name is Blessed Kateri!"

Joey thought he was minus a brother,
    Cried and clung to his mother,
Father "Sal," took him for a treat,
    So he would not be so bleak!

Heartbeat pounded...did almost cease,
    "Must we notify the police?"
Suddenly before my demise,
    Entered Peter...NO DISGUISE!

From the bus, what Allan was seeing,
    An image of Peter...hard believing,
Not long on bus "64,"
    Soon he dashed out the door!

Ran faster than a ram,
    Catching up with his LOST LAMB,
"Peter, Peter, where were YOU?"
    We looked and looked until BLUE!"

"You were beginning to cause us worry,
    Why didn't you see the 'carabinieri!'
"Being lost was sufficient trouble,
    Communication would be rubble!"

"A little prayer to Kateri,
    Then like a wind l did flee,
Kept right on moving...never gave up,
    Hope l'm not too late for sup!"

The Nord did rock with happy cheers,
    His safe return dispelled all fears,
Peter's baby brother "Joe,"
    Hugged him...wouldn't let him go!

While mother caressed her errant son,
    Listened intently to a wise nun,
"In the temple, Christ was sent,
    Peter, too...his time was spent!"

"One thing if l may suggest,
    To guarantee an identity test,"
Our friend Helen did exclaim,
    "Wearing tags with address and name!"

Uttered "daddy" with "esprit de corps,"
    "On them, we'll write in words galore,
'Dear St. Anthony...to the Nord return,
    This lost article for whom we yearn!' "

After a prayer in appreciation,
    Left the hotel for satiation!
Took our friends for a Roman treat,
    Many others did we meet!

Carrying binoculars and camera cases...

Daddy Allan & Joseph at Coliseum

A Day at the Sistine Chapel
June 23, 1980

Alarm went off, mother did wake,
    Realizing a hopeless fate,
All the Mc Cauleys almost dead,
    Would not even budge from bed!

Phone rang...a voice sang,
    "Bus is ready with the gang!"
"If an atom did explode,
    T'would not shake this sorry load!"

"Sad to be missing this liturgy,
    Honoring, Blessed Kateri,"
A major event couldn't be kept,
    While family slept...mother wept!

At ten o'clock...dad did beam,
    "Let's head for the chapel "Sistine!"
A few directives...regimental,
    Then a breakfast...Continental!

A "magic carpet," it did seem,
    By eleven...the Vatican Museum!
Carrying binoculars and camera cases,
    Peter and Joey wore happy faces!

Dad made clear that if either got lost,
    "Meet at the fountain" whatever the cost!"
First we entered a vestibule,
    With an ample supply of energy fuel!

Ascended the top by the spiral stair,
    Sistine Chapel beyond compare!
The chapel, after Pope Sixtus IV,
    Spellbound by frescoes, ceiling to floor!

Built: 1477...Chapel Sistine,
    Upon a Pope's death, majestic scene!
For new election, the doors they lock,
    Within these walls, world Cardinals flock!

From the altar through the hall,
    Old and New Testaments filled the wall!
Perugino to Botticelli,
    Ghirlandaio to Signorelli!

To Michaelangelo, let's take a look,
    The Last Judgment from the "Holy Book,"
Above the altar on the great wall,
    Enraptured, we had to stall!

Christ the Judge, dominated,
    Wherein His justice...permeated,
Immersed in apocalyptic gloom
    Of life and then "eternal doom!"

The curved vault, decorated,
    Magnificent achievement, all related,
The sun, moon and creation,
    Light and darkness...separation!

Birth and fall of Adam and Eve,
    Noah and the flood...hard to believe,
Sibyls and prophets around the scenes,
    The summit of grandeur...one deems!

Overwhelmed, Joseph did call,
    "Michaelangelo surely was TALL,
To paint so high on the ceiling wall!"
    "How come his people don't FALL?"

Gave many an explanation,
    Paradise serpent a BIG sensation!
Continued through the gallery,
    Frescoes of Raphael and Bramante.

Over Rome, Mc Cauleys...fleeing,
    The rest of the day...sightseeing!
A cozy cafe we found to eat,
    Barbecued chicken..an American treat!

A bit of wine as we did dine,
    Relaxing...happily, feeling fine!
Exhausted at our bedroom door,
    Joey collapsed on the floor!

Day was done, so was Joseph

Terrence Cardinal Cooke
with Native Americans
before Mass at the N.A. College

"Great Spirit Prayer" by Iron Eyes

Event:
Mass at the North American College
June 23 as Related to
Mc Cauleys on June 24, 1980

T'was the 24th of June, a morning bright,
    Breakfast was a sheer delight,
Talk centered on the great highlight,
    Mass at the College...moving sight!

Friends related with accuracy,
    Details of the liturgy,
Main celebrant...Cardinal Krol,
    Philadelphia's spirited soul!

Concelebration led by Cardinal Cooke,
    Eight Bishops and thirty priests, it took,
Father Egan and Monsignor Lenz,
    Led the procession of Kateri's friends.

Mass at the North American College
Photo: Anne Scheureman

Bishop Howard Hubbard Delivers Homily
at the Mass at the North American College

People described so joyfully,
  Bishop Hubbard's homily,
"From the Mohawk trail to the Tiber bank,
  A tortuous road...she made the rank!"

"For Kateri who loved the cross,
  A denial of body, to her no loss,
Full of Christ so eager to share,
  Led by her lights resplendent with prayer!"

Praised those who helped her in a special way,
  From her youth to this glorious day!
A moving speech everyone did say,
  From Heaven, a sparkling ray!

Deacon Spears

Profound joy evoked some tears,
    Gospel by Deacon Spears,
His eagle feathers did symbolize,
    The dauntless spirit of the tribes!

"Great Spirit Prayer," by Iron Eyes,
    In sign language...great surprise!
Sister Rosita's prayer of thanksgiving,
    Native Americans joined in singing!

A buffet for the clergy and laity,
    Hail...to Blessed Kateri!
A beautiful affair...recreated,
    A joyful air permeated!

Waiting for St. Anna's Gate to Open
Photo: Fr. Simon Conrad, O.F.M.

Marlene Holds Print of 'Kateri's Children of the World'
(Photo: Father Simon Conrad, O.F.M.)

Native Americans Meet with the Holy Father
June 24, 1980
Noon

To "St. Anna's gate," all did go,
    Where great joy did overflow,
Native Americans were waiting the call,
    To see their Vicar at Clementine hall!

Saw Father Béchard, Vice-Postulated,
    Near him..."Mc Cauley's Incorporated!"
Printed on Allan's shirt so RED!
    "Shows great spirit!" Father said!

Mom gave away portraits of Kateri,
    To Indian friends and clergy,
"Our Pope will bless it," some did say,
    Soon Native Americans on their way!

"McCauley's Incorporated" (Daddy Allan)

We had some lunch, spent time touring,
    Around the colonnade, exploring!
When time to meet our friends at gate,
    Saw "Billy Antone" BLUE...his fate?

Billy's tale so very sad,
    "He lost a 'treasure' that he had,
Kateri with Children, from Marlene,
    By Vatican security...last seen!"

T'was a gift to his Papago clan,
    To have Pope bless it was Billy's plan,
Came to pass...his happy dream,
    A sunny smile cross his face did beam!

Alas, ephemeral was that smile,
    For possession was Billy's for a short while,
In a flash, the guards did seize,
    The Kateri print over mournful pleas!

Pope John Paul blessed it, true,
    T'was HIS gift guards did construe!
"Just you wait, in minutes few,
    Your picture will be back to you!"

"Speak to proper authority,
      Pray to Blessed Kateri!"
Renewed hope, spirits elated,
      The Pope's talk, he related!

"Of the Saints, is Blessed Kateri,
      Interceding in HIS MERCY,
Forever helping without cease,"
      He greeted us in Christ's peace!

"We are called to holiness,
      Living in His love, spotless,"
Send my love to whomever you reach!
      T'was the essence of his speech!

Billy Antone
By Vatican security last seen...

ARRIVERDERCI ROMA!

Allan, Marlene, Joseph and Peter

Arriverderci Roma!

June 26th

The 26th of June, departure day,
    Time went too fast, some did say,
Allan left early, a package to mail,
    Said it was worse than being in jail!

Joe fell asleep on "John Henry,"
    Only minutes to be friendly!
Off to Mass, Peter did go,
    To St. Mary Major of the snow!

To St. Alphonsus, mother did tread,
    To meet a group who went ahead,
Praying that Allan would have time for Mass,
    Caught him passing his eager lass!

Thanked God for answering the prayer so fast,
    And for the memorable week that past,
Back to the Nord, suitcases to board,
    Then to Da Vinci, energy soared!

Albany Pilgrims
Photo: Anne Scheureman

A photo of the group, Anne Scheureman did take,
Mc Cauleys unseen, in the back, did make!
Waiting, waiting, the familiar tune,
"Be patient, we'll be boarding soon!"

Bishop Howard Hubbard, Joseph & Fr. Kern

Airport alive with many a vibration,
　　Clusters of people ending vacation,
Bishop Hubbard with Joseph did pose,
　　Shutters clicking, "On your toes!"

Soon the line began to flow,
　　To Father Hemauer, said, "hello!"
A pack of people on their way,
　　Taking seats without delay!

Next to Father Egan, did sit,
　　Enjoying heartily, tales of wit!
Joey using his lap for a bed,
　　Over the Atlantic, Alitalia sped!

Arrival at JFK Airport
New York
June 26th

T'was nearing the end of a hot, humid day,
    When plane landed at "JFK,"
Luggage waiting, concluding skit,
    Peter and Joey found a place to sit!

Met Father Egan's brother, "Dick,"
    Talked about a nun-friend, "sick,"
Invited Father Georges Mathieu to stay,
    Whose plane to leave the following day!

Luck never seemed to go his way,
    Suitcases, somewhere...far away!
Allan's brother, "Pete," did greet,
    This weary clan in the heat!

"Let's go home, the family to meet,
    An ice, cold BEER can't be beat!!"
This "Potawatami" priest, a delight,
    Mc Cauleys chatted with him all night!

Brought him to "JFK" by eight,
    Suitcases found, "BIG MISTAKE!"
A friend forever, we said "goodbye,"
    Father parted with spirits high!

Epilogue

The Holy Hill

Sister Mary Ignatius...sixty years a nun,
    Irish brogue...full of fun,
Of the "Infant Jesus Congregation,"
    Helping poor and contemplation
Welcoming light of Martyr's shrine,
    Worked fifty years in summertime
Our friendship began in "74,"
    Welcomed our family at manor door,
Her eyes as blue as the habit she wore!
    In charge of Jogues Manor at the shrine,
Her loving smile did always shine!
    Each year performing our Kateri show,
Her kindness, we always did know!
    A cup of tea...a rosary,
Loving tales of Kateri,
    Her happy ventures with the poor,
A child's temper, she would endure,
    Not by spanking but an Irish jig,
Until his face beamed so BIG!
    Once when our Mary had the flu,
There was much for her to do,
    Aspirin...towels and a prayer,
Soon Mary well with care.
    Time passed...six years fled by,
God...now calling her to die!

Sr. Mary Ignatius, I.J.C.

At convent infirmary on July one,
We had made a visit to this jolly nun,
    Had bone cancer but did conceal,
"Tis only a cold...a bit weak, I feel!"
    Hospital visit though brief, a delight,
Her sparkling eyes shone so bright,
    We spoke of our Blessed KATERI,
In short time, a Saint, she'll be!"
    Sister held Joseph for minutes few,
"Ignatius is your middle name,
    I, too have the same!"
With twinkle in eye and smile so dear,
    "You'll always be mine...never fear!"
Showed her photos of the family,
    "God bless each, so lovely!"
She longed to return to the "holy hill,"
    Kateri's home...Auriesville,
"By the end of July, I'll be there,"
    Peter played a jig; then we said a prayer,
The fifth glorious mystery,
    For Sister Ignatius recovery!
We took some photos, then kissed "goodbye,"
    Promising to meet on hill so high!
Our Lord works with His will divine,
    He knows when it's our time,
This dear lover of Kateri,
    On the fourth glorious mystery,
Entered God's eternal light,
    July 25th reached her height!

Sr. Mary Ignatius, I.J.C. with Julia Egan

A week before to her surprise,
 Her friend Julia Egan's sudden demise,
Son, Father Egan, saw signification,
 Both women to Kateri, a special affection,
Chosen by God, the grandest selection,
 To walk on each side, hand in hand,
With their Blessed Kateri through Heavenland,
 Awaiting the next grand celebration,
The "Lily of the Mohawk's" canonization!
 Precious memories will linger on,
Now must sing our parting song,
 "Thank you, Blessed Kateri,"
Time to say, "Arriverderci!"
 With our heart and soul, we'll pray,
Your sainthood...not far away,
 For now we'll say "farewell" until,
We call you "Saint" on "holy hill!"

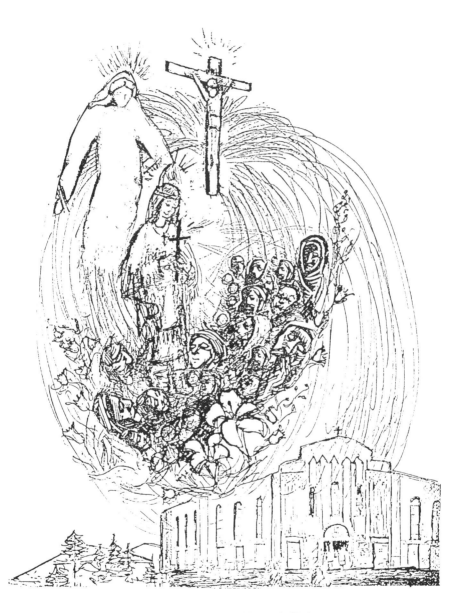

North American Martyr's Shrine
Auriesville, N.Y.
"Holy Hill"

Brother Raymond W. Bounds, S.J. holding Peter Ross

September 27, 1981

Dear Allan, Marlene, Francis X, Mary, Anne,
    Tom, Peter and Joey:

I just visited Rome and certainly enjoyed the trip. (The days are to
be treasured and are in print.) It was a jam pack trip with many
important things to witness and enjoy. It was a family affair
enjoyed with many friends; a day of honor to a little Indian maid.
The trip was truly enjoyed and we give thanks that Peter who was
lost in the shuffle was found. We also give thanks to God for a safe
trip. So we are now back home enjoying the continued family joys
of life. Yep, I made a trip to Rome and enjoyed it very much.

                    Pax Christi!
                    Love to All!

                    Bro. Ray
                    Brother Ray

Br. Raymond Bounds, S.J.
went to heaven April 23, 1992

PART IV

LATER DAYS: ROME TO HOME

Marlene McCauley,
Wearing Kateri Necklace

Part IV

Later Days: Rome to Home

Christ said, "The humble shall be exhalted." The humble, shy little Kateri must have hidden behind a golden cloud in Heaven, with all the attention being focused on her throughout the world. During her longhouse days, Kateri would blush under her shawl, hiding herself like a turtle under its shell, if the least bit of fuss was made over her. Kateri attained the honors of the altar and the enthusiasm which followed from Rome to home, spread its wings in a resurgence of devotion caressing every aspect of society with unbelievable magnitude. Father Francis X. Weiser, S.J. (our family's spiritual director, referred to in "Early Days"), wrote that he offered his first official Mass in tribute to "our beloved little Saint," the day of her beatification, a realization of a life-long dream.

Within days, Kateri's name became a household word to the entire world's Catholic community. Kateri became patroness of camps, hospitals, orphanages, schools, centers and organizations; newborns and confirmation candidates also were named after Kateri. The exciting adventures of life in the Eastern woodland came alive in the classroom as the fascinating tale of Blessed Kateri's life was related to spellbound youngsters. The youth instantly fell in love with her, forming "Kateri" clubs, cookie kitchens and even naming pets after her. A young senorita from Spain wrote hymns which told the story of the Indian maiden. Soon, thereafter, cars were seen sporting Kateri license plates. Following the wildfire spread of her devotion, petitions of all kinds were being granted to young and old alike, ranging from the granting of simple favors to the curing of serious maladies.

The Vice-Postulators of the United States and Canada, Fathers Joseph McBride, S.J. and Henri Béchard, S.J., respectively, were deluged with mail requests for more information about Kateri. Their subscriptions to the *Lily* and *Kateri* magazines skyrocketed. Membership of the National Tekakwitha Conference, an organization for the Catholic native peoples of North America, continued to multiply to enormous proportions. While Kateri worked around the heavenly clock to help souls on earth, her friends here worked around their earthly timepieces, doing everything within their power that could aid her cause for canonization.

Father Béchard was happy to relate in a letter of May, 1981, that a new commemorative stamp was launched by the Canadian government and four Bishops attended the glorious event at the mission. Kateri would have FLED far into the woods at this type of honor!

A letter of Nov. 1981, from Father Béchard, reveals the growth of the Kateri devotion since her beatification. An excerpt follows:

> "Since the beatification, interest in Blessed Kateri has grown considerably. Indians, in particular are happy that one of them has been elevated to the glory of the altars. Now they are looking forward to her canonization. That's why, I'm trying to get 50,000 signed pledges of a daily "Our Father" and "Hail Mary" for the canonization of the "Lily of the Mohawks."

The crowning glory came when upon her beatification, Kateri was officially added to the Church calendar. Traditionally, upon beatification, the new Blessed's feast day would be the day of her death, (April 17, in Kateri's case). In 1983, it was changed by the Holy See's commission at the urging of Father McBride and the New York Bishops led by Bishop Howard Hubbard of Albany, Episcopal head of the Kateri cause. This new date, July 14, coincided with the height of the Summer activities honoring Kateri at her Auriesville shrine, as well as avoided conflicting with Holy Week services. Canada kept the original feast day, April 17.

How thrilling it was for all! One friend, Mary Callary, wrote:

> "What a surprise to see Kateri's feast day in the Mass booklet. Let us pray that she will be declared a "Saint" soon.

> Providentially, a lily plant which had been discarded in my yard since Spring, had bloomed in my Cape Cod kitchen in front of Kateri's picture on July 14. Friends visiting us, couldn't get over it."

A monumental leap in the history of the Catholic Church occurred when Pope John Paul II, selected Fathers Donald E. Pelotte, S.S.S. of the Abenaki nation (1986) and Charles Joseph Chaput, O.F.M.Cap., a Potawatami (1988) as the first Native American Bishops. These were great moments for the Indians of the United States and Canada and surely must have made Kateri smile from Heaven for they would help to hasten her canonization. In a letter to Father Béchard, Bishop Charles Chaput wrote:

> "The canonization of Bl. Kateri is in my prayers daily."

Bishop Donald Pelotte said to Pope John Paul during his visit to Phoenix, Arizona, Sept. 14, 1987:

> "We thank you for the beatification of our sister in faith, Bl. Kateri Tekakwitha. We prayerfully await the day when the Church publicly celebrates her as, Saint Kateri Tekakwitha."

In response, our dear Holy Father gently smiled and softly nodded his head.

Relative to Bishop Pelotte's good word for Kateri, Father Béchard, wrote in the Spring *Kateri,* 1988:

> "Much applause greeted Bishop Donald Pelotte as he began to welcome the Pope. A thunderous applause followed when he called for the canonization of Bl. Kateri Tekakwitha, "Lily of the Mohawk."

Kateri's friends never lost an opportunity to promote her saintly qualities. During the address of Pima Indian, Alfretta Antone to the Holy Father when he visited Phoenix in 1987, she praised Kateri as a beautiful example of a native person living the Christian gospel. She added that through Kateri's help, her people were being gathered to the Church.

During the Pope's several visits to the Canadian missions and Indian reservations, (1984 and 1987) he heard constant affirmation of Kateri's greatly beneficial impact upon all Native peoples. Pope John Paul's love for Kateri was apparent during his Canadian visits. At Sainte Anne de Beaupre, September 10, 1984, he declared:

> "I recall that beautiful day when Kateri Tekakwitha was beatified in Rome where some of you were present."

At Huronia, Ontario, September 15, of the same year, he stated:

> "A young woman of Algonquin and Mohawk ancestry also deserves special recognition today: Blessed Kateri Tekakwitha. Who has not heard of her outstanding witness of purity and holiness of life? It was my personal joy, only four years ago, to beatify this woman of great courage and faith, who is known by many as the "Lily of the Mohawks." To those who came to Rome for her beatification, I said:

> 'Blessed Kateri stands before us as a symbol of the heritage that is yours as North American Indians' (June 24, 1980)!

In 1985, the McCauleys had the joy of attending our Holy Father's Mass at Castel Gandolfo, after which we presented him with a video of our family's puppet show production, "Lily of the Mohawks" with a note gently nudging our wonderful Pope to canonize Kateri. While "Mama Marlene" kissed the Pope's cheek, she said a little prayer:

"Please dear Kateri, nudge our dear Pope to make you a Saint!"

When "Daddy Allan" was informed later, he exclaimed to his bridey: "You should be the patron saint of GENTLE NUDGING!"

Great news from our nation's capitol... Msgr. Paul A. Lenz is happy to announce that a life-sized white marble statue of Blessed Kateri will fill the last available niche of the Basilica of the National Shrine of the Immaculate Conception in Washington, D.C. and will be blessed during a gathering of the Bishops of the United States in November, 1992.

Pray that Kateri's influence will help to restore the great spiritual values upon which America was founded.

Marlene presenting the McCauley Family's video production of "Lily of The Mohawks" to the Holy Father, Castel Gandolfo, Italy, 1985

KATERI PRAYER

O God, who among the many marvels of Your Grace in the New World, did cause to blossom on the banks of the Mohawk and of the St. Lawrence, the pure and tender Lily, Kateri Tekakwitha, grant we beseech You, the favor we beg through her intercession; (your request) that this Young Lover of Jesus and of His Cross may soon be counted among the Saints of Holy Mother Church, and that our hearts may be enkindled with a stronger desire to imitate her innocence and faith. Through the same Christ Our Lord. Amen.

Our Father and Hail Mary once, and Glory be to the Father, three times.

IMPRIMATUR: Most Rev. Bishop Howard Hubbard, D.D.

Trukese Children with Kateri
Photo: Rev. Ronald Sams, S.J.

End of Adventures

The journey has ended. May you continue to walk with Kateri through life, ever following her beautiful example of faith, love of Christ and deep devotion to mankind, which will surely produce joy and peace in your life.

Amen.

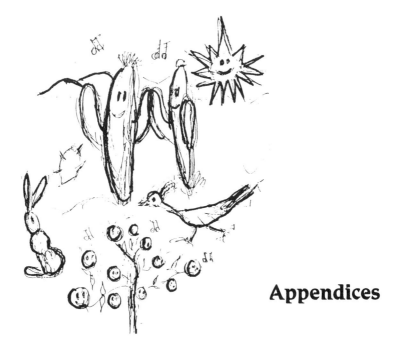

Appendices

Marlene and Allan

Biography of Author

As early as she could remember, Marlene McCauley wanted to be an actress. Her earliest performances took place under the backyard apple tree and later relocated to the family's basement, a part of which had been converted into a theatre by the use of sheets, blankets and a makeshift curtain. Her mother pulled the curtain and her dad was ticket collector and prop man. These performances continued, becoming increasingly sophisticated, ultimately resulting in a scholarship to Curry College, Milton, Mass. and a Dramatic Arts Degree, followed by more theatre experience at Emmanuel College, Boston, Mass., at the same time taking an English and Art Degree.

Before going to New York, Marlene's mom warned her that the "Big Apple" was a dangerous place; it was for this reason that she decided to board with Hungarian nuns, attending 5:00 a.m. Mass daily, while operating under a midnight curfew, locked gates and all! Her acting career developed right on schedule, for within a short time, she managed an audition with Lee Strasberg at Actor's Studio, which went very well and led to another company for additional experience which was highly regarded by Lee. The experience came but so did an experience of a different kind.....

For a diversion from the hectic pace of New York, Marlene dated occasionally with no intention of getting side-tracked from her career; God had other plans! It was a cold, rainy, windy February morning in New York City and being chilled to her bones, Marlene entered the Majestic cafeteria on Broadway for a warm cup of coffee. A charming Irishman followed Marlene out of the restaurant. On August 24, 1992, and six children later, they will have celebrated their 35th wedding anniversary!

"A Happy Circus"
Front row, left to right: Francis X with "Puff", the Lamb,
Anne (Tinkle Bell, the Elf), Tom More (Rudolph).
Back row: Mary (Christmas Fairy), Marlene (Popcorn, the Clown)
holding Angel Peter.

Following this eventful meeting, it became apparent that Marlene and her new friend had in common all the things that really mattered: similar goals in life, the same values, a love and devotion to family, a very strong religious conviction and above all, a great love of God. Although this "charmer" piqued Marlene's interest, she was still concerned that this chance meeting could present a stumbling block to her career. It was for this reason that an offer to join Ringling Bros. Circus as a performer, requiring relocation to Sarasota, Florida for extended training was accepted. This was a great opportunity for her to put their own friendship in proper perspective. Florida proved to be a delightful experience but the emotional embers did not die, for the couple were in constant written contact and upon the Big Top's arrival in New York City, Allan attended every perform ance, seated in the first row next to Ted Evans, the sideshow giant, so he could be spotted easily by his performer pal, perched atop "Ruthie," her elephant! Marlene also danced, did a comedy act with Otto Griebling, the sad clown and sketched backstage in spare time. After a short time on the road, Marlene finally became Allan's shining star, for they were married in the St. Malachy's, Actor's Chapel by circus priest, Father "Ed" Sullivan with Father Francis X. Weiser, S.J. concelebrating, August 24, 1957. After the Nuptial Mass, the wedding party rode a horse and buggy through Central Park. Later, Allan told Marlene, "You can't get the circus out of your blood!" Life for the McCauleys has been a "circus" ever since!

Before the first child was born, Marlene taught art in the Amityville, Long Island school system where she introduced the art of puppetry. Fascinated with this form of creative expression which combined art and drama, Marlene gave birth to the "Popcorn Puppet Playhouse," along with her first newborn, Francis Xavier. Francis Xavier was born on the feast of this great Jesuit Saint and baptized by Father Francis Xavier Weiser, who happened to be visiting his publisher in New York at the time. With the advent of the family's theatre, and several children later, the "Circus on Strings," a puppet-moppet act with marionettes, was created with Francis Xavier as the Master of Ceremonies and each child playing a clown charac- ter as he or she became old enough to toddle!

After performing for department stores, libraries and museums in New York City, the family was invited to present their "Circus," at the World's Fair in 1965. Following the show, a feature article appeared in the *New York Daily News,* describing Mama Marlene as the "Phyllis Diller of Motherhood!" Other articles appeared in publications which encouraged the McCauleys to continue their "Circus" in Phoenix, Arizona where they moved for Marlene's health, in 1965. By then, Allan had his Law Degree. The "Circus" appeared on "Kid's World," national television in the mid- seventies. Added to the repetoire were seasonal and religious shows, such as, "Miracle of the Roses" and "Fatima Story." Allan became the show's Director, Actor, Prop-man and Jack-of-all-Mundane-Tasks.

Following son Peter's hearing cure by Kateri's intercession, "Lily of the Mohawks," was written. The show was performed all over the United States, in Daddy Allan's spare time, from Capistrano Mission in California to the Shrine of the North American Martyrs in Auriesville, New York, where the McCauley family received the Kateri award for 1975. Added to the cast was Joseph Ignatius as 'Babe Kateri' born after much prayer and a novena to Kateri. He came just in time for the tri-centennial celebration of Kateri's baptism, July 31, 1976, feast of St. Ignatius, founder of the Jesuit Order. Three day old Joseph Ignatius was the youngest delegate at the Eucharistic Congress in Philadelphia and baptized at the "Old St. Joseph's Church," shortly after his performance!

In 1985, at Castel Gandolfo, Italy, the McCauley family presented Pope John Paul II with their video production of "Lily of the Mohawks." This meeting was a highlight of their lives. Presently in 1992, with three children off to College, two married and only Joseph, age 15, home full time, Marlene has had the needed time to lecture and write this little book, conveying to others about the wonders of her little friend, "Kateri Tekakwitha," so they too could come to know and love her. Marlene is now completing a biography of Kateri for children to be published soon.

McCauley Family with Pope John Paul II

Bibliography

Béchard, S.J., Fr. Henri, *The Original Caughnawaga Indians*, International Publishers, Montreal, Canada, 1976.

Béchard, S.J., Fr. Henri, *Kateri Quarterly*, Kateri Center, Kahnawake, Quebec.

McBride, S.J., Joseph, *Lily Publication*, Tekakwitha League, Auriesville, New York.

Thwaites, Reuben G., *Jesuit Relations and Allied Documents*, ed., Cleveland, 1896-1901, 73 Vols.

The Venerable Servant of God, Kateri Tekakwitha, Positio of the Historical Section of the Sacred Congregation of Rites, Rome, English Edition, New York, 1940.

Weiser, S.J., Francis X., *Kateri Tekakwitha*, Kateri Center, Kahnawake, P.Q., Canada, 1972.

Statements of the present two Vice-Postulators of Kateri Tekakwitha's cause, reveal the urgency of your prayers to attain the miracle needed for her canonization. They are as follows:

"An URGENT Message"
Rev. Jacques Bruyère, S.J.
Vice-Postulator of Canada

The canonization of Kateri Tekakwitha would be a tremendous benefit to us all in these difficult times, especially to our beloved Native Americans who are making a wonderful effort to blend their culture with the faith in order to realize the birth of a magnificently beautiful native spirituality. Kateri can be their guiding star.

When we reflect that Kateri too, was a lay person who endured all the struggles and temptations of this life, she serves as an outstanding example of purity, virtue and devotion to God and her fellow man...someone we may all emulate.

Let us pray one "Our Father," one "Hail Mary" and three "Glory Be's," daily for her sainthood.

"A Plea for Kateri"
U.S. Vice Postulator
Fr. John J. Paret, S.J.
Auriesville, New York
1-92

I know you are praying, but I have to ask you to redouble your prayers that Kateri will "make it" in the near future. I'm sure it would be such a blessing for the entire American Church, and certainly for our Native American friends. We have to keep reminding ourselves that in the final analysis, it is in the hands of God. But Jesus said, "Ask and you shall receive," and what we are asking seems to be eminently worth asking for! So let's keep up our prayers with confidence.

For further information on her cause: Sincerely in Christ,

Kateri Center
St. Francis Xavier Mission   John J. Paret, S.J.
CP 70
Kahnawake, P.Q.
JOL 1BO
Quebec, Canada

In the United States: **National Kateri Center**
Auriesville, N.Y
12016

Kateri Shrines

KATERI'S BIRTHPLACE
Auriesville, N.Y. 12016
National Kateri Center
Tekakwitha League Headquarters
Office of the Vice-Postulator
National Shrine of the North American Martyrs

KATERI'S BAPTISIMAL SITE
Fonda, N.Y. 12068
Tekakwitha Memorial Chapel
Mohawk Indian Museum
Restored Mohawk Village of Caughnawaga

KATERI'S TOMB
Kahnawake, P.Q.
C.P. 70
Quebec, Canada; JOL, IBO
St. Francis Xavier Mission Church
Home of World-Renowned Mohawk Choir
Office of the Canadian Vice-Postulator

To Order

ADVENTURES WITH A SAINT:
Kateri Tekakwitha, "Lily of The Mohawks"

— Marlene McCauley —

Please mail
$9.95 plus $2.00 for
handling and mailing
(add $1.00 for each additional book)
Special Discount for Bulk Orders

To: Grace House Publishing
6237 N. 15th Street
Phoenix, Arizona 85014
(602) 265-9151
(602) 994-9902